The Science *of the* Rishis

"Vanamali's writing is a *Pancajanya,* inviting all *bharatas* to bask in the luminous wisdom of their venerable heritage. Mataji's writing is a divinely inspired, ecstatic pilgrimage to the feet of India's great *rishis.* Vanamali passionately illuminates the rishis liberating revelations as the Himalayan summit of human consciousness, with an unparalleled power to transform men and women into gods and goddesses!"

BRUCE BURGER, FOUNDER OF HEARTWOOD INSTITUTE AND AUTHOR OF *ESOTERIC ANATOMY: THE BODY AS CONSCIOUSNESS*

"*The Science of the Rishis* is informative, inspirational, and a compelling read. I would recommend it to any serious student of Hinduism as well as a casual reader who is trying to broaden his knowledge."

GOPINATH PILLAI, AMBASSADOR AT LARGE, MINISTRY OF FOREIGN AFFAIRS, SINGAPORE

"Vanamali is an outstanding teacher of Vedanta and an eminent scholar having dedicated her entire life for the cause of Sanatana Dharma. The book is a treasure for posterity."

RAMA NARAYANAN, PRIVATE SECRETARY TO CHAIRMAN, PUBLIC ACCOUNTS COMMITTEE PARLIAMENT OF INDIA

D1554951

Sri Ganeshaaya Namaha!

Salutations to Lord Ganesha!
Who removes and overcomes all obstacles,
And grants success in every endeavor.

GANASHTAKAM

The Science *of the* Rishis

The Spiritual and Material Discoveries of the Ancient Sages of India

Vanamali

Inner Traditions
Rochester, Vermont • Toronto, Canada

Inner Traditions
One Park Street
Rochester, Vermont 05767
www.InnerTraditions.com

Text stock is SFI certified

Library of Congress Cataloging-in-Publication Data

Vanamali, 1935– author.
 [Science called Hinduism]
 The science of the rishis : the spiritual and material discoveries of the ancient sages of India / Vanamali.
   pages cm
 Originally published in India in 2013 by Aryan Books International under the title The science called Hinduism.
 Includes bibliographical references and index.
 ISBN 978-1-62055-386-2 (paperback) — ISBN 978-1-62055-387-9 (e-book)
 1. Hinduism. 2. Hinduism and science. I. Title.
 BL1202.V36 2015
 294.5'2—dc23

2014032152

Printed and bound in the United States by Lake Book Manufacturing, Inc.
The text stock is SFI certified. The Sustainable Forestry Initiative® program promotes sustainable forest management.

10 9 8 7 6 5 4 3 2 1

Text design and layout by Priscilla Baker
This book was typeset in Garamond Premier Pro with Kingsbury and Gill Sans as display fonts

To send correspondence to the author of this book, mail a first-class letter to the author c/o Inner Traditions • Bear & Company, One Park Street, Rochester, VT 05767, and we will forward the communication, or contact the author directly at **www.vanamaliashram.org**.

ॐ

Dharmaaya Namaha!
Salutations to the Eternal Law!

❦

Dedicated to
My dearest brother, friend, and companion,
Mohan—
With deep gratitude for the innumerable ways
he has served Vanamali for so many years.
Without him Vanamali Ashram would not function.

Bharat Mata

Awake O Mother!
The time has come to assert your rights!
To open the veil of ages,
To disclose your eyes,
Filled with the wisdom of the ages,
Your children are crying to Thee,
Why are you silent?
Queen of Beauty!
Queen of Wisdom!
Queen of the World!
Uplift us who have fallen so low
As to put artha before dharma,
Who have renounced moksha
And embraced kama.
Help us, O mother!
Deliver us from the greed that seems to bind us,
Allow us to raise our heads once again
And proclaim to the world,
This is our land!
The Holy Land!
The land of the sages!
The land of martyrs!
The land that has given the world
The knowledge of our Immortal Self,
The knowledge to free us
From the thrall of ignorance.

Contents

ॐ

Essentials of Hinduism

Is Hinduism or Sanatana Dharma a religion, as such? Religion generally denotes a system of morality based on the concept of God. Sanatana Dharma is not something exclusively like that. It evolved in the Gangetic plains in prehistoric times, when the world had not seen or heard the word *religion* at all. To speak then of Hinduism or Sanatana Dharma as a religion is, to say the least, preposterous. But sometimes such references and statements do creep into the minds of people, and it becomes difficult to correct them.

This does not mean that no efforts should be made to amend such misperceptions. In fact, any society remains vibrant and creative only when it hosts thinkers who examine the misunderstandings and delusions of people from time to time and effectively administer corrective measures. We cannot blame any society for its wrongs. But it is inexcusable indeed if its thinking members do not take stock of the situation and strive to remedy them.

The word *dharma* does not have an English equivalent, although *righteousness* can be an approximate word to convey what *dharma* stands for. *Dharma* denotes the power or process of sustaining human life in all situations, in fortune and misfortune, favor and disfavor, prosperity and adversity. This power is truly applicable to the mind and intelligence, not to anything else in the human personality.

The word *Hindu* also calls for a discreet analysis and assessment. Barhaspatya Samhita (a section of the *Rig Veda*) defines it as the land lying between the Himalayas to the north and Indusarovara (the Indian Ocean) to the south. The relevant verse reads thus:

हिमालयात्समारभ्य यावदिन्दुसरोवरम् ।
तद्देवनिर्मितं देशं हिन्दुस्थानं प्रचक्षते ॥

Beginning from the Himalayas extending to Indusarovara, the land created by the Lord is called Hindusthanam, the word being derived from the first letter of "Himalaya" and the last letter of "Indu." Those who belong to Hindusthanam are called "Hindu."

Hindu, thus, is not a religious name. It is a territorial or geographical reference, denoting the people who lived and still live in a specific area of the earth. Whatever new religion or cult they belong to does not matter at all. They are all ethnically Hindus, having been born in and continuing to live in this blessed land.

The concept, process, and pursuit of righteousness were evolved by the dwellers in Hindusthanam, who lived and spread in the plains, graced by the perennial flow of the holy river. We cannot say when the thought process and culture first began. As we are not able to trace any point of time when this transpired, it has naturally come to be regarded as *anadi,* or beginningless.

It also can be said to be without end. Over the ages, an amazing assortment of literature has evolved on the theme of dharma. Even now all the scriptural writings on Sanatana Dharma have not been traced. The fact that these are too numerous to be identified is clearly revealed by a proverbial statement:

अनन्तशास्त्रं बहु वेदितव्यं
स्वल्पश्च कालो बहवश्च विघ्ना: ।

यत्सारभूतं तदुपासितव्यं
हंसैर्यथा क्षीरमिवाम्बुमिश्रम् ॥

Scriptural compositions are endless. There is a great deal to be known. The obstacles are many, but the time available is short. Therefore, the essence of all these must be discerned and pursued vigorously, like swans separating milk mixed with water.

Swans reputedly have the unique capacity to separate milk from water and drink it exclusively. Such is the art and process of discrimination the dharmic votary must have, in approaching the countless scriptures Sanatana Dharma encompasses.

The dharmic thoughts and practices of this land have been presented in various forms to guide people to navigate the ocean of Hindu scriptures and understand the relevance of their fundamental tenets and pursuits. Sage Valmiki's *Ramayana,* Vyasadeva's *Mahabharatam, Srimad Bhagavatam,* and many other such writings have been evolved to serve the purpose of presenting the thoughts with a renewed concern and relevance to life. Sanatana Dharma has continued to be a subject of wide exposition. Spiritual and philosophical discourses form part of the Hindu culture and tradition. Enlightening discourses are widely attended by both the erudite and common people, young as well as old. Efforts like these should continue. Only then will the newer generations have the opportunity to know the continuing relevance of this most ancient spiritual-philosophical analysis of human life and the resultant guidance as to how it leads to success, peace, and fulfillment.

COMPREHENSIVE SCRIPTURAL VISION ABOUT LIFE AND SOCIETY

The uniqueness of Sanatana Dharma is that the same basic spiritual and philosophical notes can be found in every form of its practice and exposition. At the same time, it is also empirical in every way. The whole dharma is phased in a very effective manner to facilitate progress and evolution. It has two phases, *achara* and *vichara*. *Achara* denotes various kinds of practices relating to individual, family, society, and the administration that governs them. *Vichara* denotes truthful introspection on these and allied matters. The intention is to begin with achara, which alone will be possible for children and young people. Then, the maturing adult should turn to meaningful introspection, or vichara, and elevate the practices from the sensory level to the mind and intelligence. In the human, the mind and intelligence are the causal factors in all activities, and they are the highest. If the sensory practice has, for example, 1 unit effect, an oral practice has 100 units, while those of the mind and the intelligence have 1,000 units and 100,000 units, respectively. Progress from one to the other is facilitated by the right exposure and guidance. People generally lack this. All the dharmic exponents strive to bridge this gap.

Despite the vast nature of Hindu literature on the subject of dharma, the concept as well as pursuit of the whole Sanatana Dharma can be condensed in three sets of four words each—a total of twelve words:

1. Four *varnas*—*braahmana, kshatriya, vaishya,* and *shudra*
2. Four *purushaarthas* (human pursuits)—*dharma, artha, kama,* and *moksha*
3. Four *ashramas*—*brahmacharya, garhasthya, vanaprastha,* and *sannyasa*

Four Varnas

Varnas refer to a fourfold inner classification of the activities and proclivities of humans. Each is necessary for the society's cohesion and welfare. The varna variety is an inevitable expression of Nature. We have no option in the matter. Instead, we should understand, assess, and be governed by it to properly lead our life and aspirations to the destined goals.

Because these are invisible, each is explained with its identification marks. For instance, regulation of desire, control of senses, austerity, cleanliness, tolerance, and straightforwardness are the traits that make the *braahmana* group. Braahmanas are generally calm and given to a life of self-restraint, inner excellence, and joy.

Kshatriyas are extrovert in nature, but chivalrous. They have such qualities and inspirations that keep societal behavior under check and balance. Heroism, valor, will, skillfulness, not retreating from battle, being given to ample charity, gifting, the feeling of lordliness—these are the traits of the kshatriya or warrior group.

Agriculture, rearing cows, dealing in trade, commerce, and industry are the predilections of the *vaishya* group. And the fourth group, *shudras,* has the predilection to be ready and willing to serve others, using their bodily resources and skill.

Fourfold Purushaarthas

What should be the goal to be achieved by members of each of these groups during their tenure upon earth? Sanatana Dharma has very clear thoughts and assessments. Our dharmic proponents have evolved the fourfold human pursuit: *dharma, artha, kama,* and *moksha.*

By *dharma* is meant the code of righteousness, which should govern the life and activities of everyone. It is all the disciplines, inspirations, restraints, and obligations necessary to blend and fuse individual life with the societal one, to make a beautiful whole.

In such a righteous life, everyone should find and develop their own monetary resources. Thus the second object is *artha,* meaning financial sufficiency. Wealth earned by one's own effort is the best, most desirable. That gained from patrimony comes next. That derived from marriage in the form of dowry and the like is derogatory.

By self-earned wealth, one must try to fulfill his legitimate desires, *kama.* Stinginess or miserliness is detestable. Frugality is the ideal, the right option. The true objective of wealth is to gain dharma, for that alone will lead to inner spiritual enlightenment, bestowing peace, wisdom, and freedom in the end.

When dharma, artha, and kama are pursued in their right order and measure, the fourth object, *moksha,* becomes relevant, facile, and meaningful. *Moksha* denotes the release from the suffocating shackles of the mind and intelligence. With such release, or redemption, one becomes heir to immortality and inner ecstasy. This is to be achieved while living here and now. Everything about dharma is thus relevant to our life, to be pursued wholesomely here and now. It enriches, empowers, enlightens, and fulfills human life.

Hindu dharma is called *sanatana* or eternal for two reasons. *Sanatanam karoti iti sanatanah.* It makes its votary feel and realize that his personality is, in truth, immortal. He is not the body. He only *has* his body, like he has his house or car. The "presence and power" that animate the body are not physical but spiritual. Different from matter and energy, which constitute the body, he is actually unborn, undying, eternal, and everywhere present. The inner consciousness that he verily is makes him immortal.

Equally so, Hindu dharma is eternal because it relates to the mind and intelligence of the human, which have not changed over ages. The ancient human had the same emotional mind and rational intelligence as his modern counterpart. Values that relate to these changeless constituents of the human personality are naturally eternal.

The scientific nature of Sanatana Dharma rests upon the observations our senses make, and the inferences the mind and intelligence arrive at on the basis of such observations. In fact, these are the two canons on which all objective sciences also rely. That objective science uses instruments like the telescope and microscope makes no difference to the fundamental nature and validity of both science and spirituality. The parts of a person that employ the instruments are one's senses. And it is the mind and intelligence within that employ the senses. Thus the grounds on which objective science and Sanatana Dharma, the subjective science, rest are exactly the same.

Sanatana Dharma lays down a set of common disciplines for all people, despite their bodily or inner differences. They are:

अहिंसा सत्यमस्तेयं शौचमिन्द्रियनिग्रह: ।
एतत्सामासिकं धर्मं चातुर्वर्ण्येऽब्रवीन्मनु: ॥

Nonhurting, not to mention nonkilling, truthfulness, nonsteal-
ing, cleanliness, and sensory control are the common disciplines
and values meant for all categories of people.

Four Ashramas or Stages in Life

To gain the fourfold purushaarthas, our dharmic exponents evolved
a four-phased life-pattern. *Brahmacharya,* celibacy and being solely
devoted to learning, is the first phase, where the student lives in the
residence of the teacher and pursues learning wholesomely. At the end
of this phase, he has the freedom to return home, get married, and raise
a family to perpetuate the lineage. He has also the choice, depending
upon the degree of dispassion and earnestness he gains, to pursue spiritual wisdom exclusively, to take directly to ascetic life, *sannyasa.*

But the second phase, household life or *garhasthya,* is not a lifelong
pursuit. At the age of 55 or 60, when one's children become adults,
one should entrust the household to them and adopt the *vanaprastha*
way of life, the third phase, devoted to truthful introspection leading
to inner refinement and expansion. This can be done along with one's
wife, if she so desires and is ready to take up the same mission of inner
refinement.

If one succeeds in fulfilling this phase, he can adopt the last phase
called *sannyasa,* renunciation, which is the climax and crowning glory
of human life. Sannyasa is a sequel to realizing one's own Imperishable
Self. *Jnanadeva kaivalya praaptih,* so goes the aphorism: "From wisdom alone dawn the joy and fulfillment of inner spiritual freedom."

Thus the twelve words, taken together, become the synopsis of
Sanatana Dharma. No matter what tendencies one has, there is a
way of changing them for the better, by adopting and practicing the
higher disciplines and values. Practice makes one perfect. In fact,
the sole object of human will and ingenuity is to change, correct,

and improve oneself, so as to become what one verily aspires for.

All four varnas have equal freedom and opportunity to adopt the four-phase life and reach the climax of fulfillment, though by nature all do not do so. Failure does not invalidate the concept of fourfold purushaartha and the sure way of achieving it.

KNOWLEDGE—THREE CATEGORIES

The school of Indian philosophy known as Vedanta ascertained ages ago that knowledge is of three kinds—*pratyaksha, paroksha,* and *aparoksha. Pratyaksha* is that knowledge gained by the sensory organs. *Paroksha* is what is arrived at by the intelligence, through inference. In these, either senses work or the mind and intelligence work.

There is another level and kind of knowledge called *aparoksha,* a concept unique to Sanatana Dharma. It is beyond the realm of senses (pratyaksha) or intelligence (paroksha). Yet there is full comprehension. For instance, how do we know that we slept and did not know anything at all? In sleep, we are unaware of the body, mind, intelligence, and even the ego. Yet we wake up to say we were, and we slept. Naturally that knowledge is beyond and different from that perceived through senses, mind, and intelligence.

It is always good to remember the fundamental principle, namely rationality, which governs Sanatana Dharma, in every step.

युक्तियुक्तं प्रगृह्णीयात् बालादपि विचक्षण: ।
अन्यत्-तु तृणवत्त्याज्यं-अप्युक्तं पद्मयोनिना ॥

The wise one should accept whatever is reasonable, told even by a child. Anything otherwise, even if stated by Brahma, the Creator, is to be summarily rejected like a blade of grass.

If this is the basic premise governing Sanatana Dharma, is there a question or doubt as to whether it is rational, scientific, and logical? In fact, there are three tests for any dharmic statement or revelation. It should be enunciated in the ageless scriptures (*shruti*); it must have the support of reason (*yukti*); and it should also be experienced by oneself (*anubhava*). Only when these three together confirm a proposition can it be accepted and followed.

WHY HINDUS WORSHIP SO MANY GODS

Though Sanatana Dharma is primarily and ultimately philosophical and spiritual, it does comprehend religious thoughts and the assorted needs of humanity and caters to varied tendencies and predilections. As in the matter of food, dress, and residences, in religious and devotional relish also there is need for ample variety. On this basis, the Hindu pantheon also arrays a variety of gods and goddesses, each of whom is imbued with a specific set of qualities, which are, in fact, the desires, choices, and affinities of the human mind. Nevertheless, Sanatana Dharma clarifies, emphasizes, and confirms in unambiguous terms that God is but one, omnipresent, having no physical form or shape.

Such a God naturally becomes unthinkable and inaccessible to ordinary minds. At the same time, no one can be denied the freedom and scope to worship God and derive the resultant benefits. This is how various deities, together with the specific qualities associated with them, have come to be evolved, sought, and spread among the people. It is more a sociopsychological compulsion than otherwise!

To give one instance, Hanuman is a pet lord of a large multitude. The *Hanuman Chaleesa,* forty hymns on Hanuman, is sung daily by millions of people. When reciting this composition with fervor and piety, the singer is infused with the qualities of Hanuman—courage, resolve, fidelity to the Master, wisdom, robust health, sensitivity, dexterity in speech, and the like. Those seeking these qualities piously sing the *Chaleesa,* thereby imbibing the essence of what they sing. In fact, all devotional practices are like this, self-enriching and self-empowering!

The best explanation about worship and its scientific background is in *Srimad Bhagavatam,* a full authority on devotion and God, where young Prahlada praises Lord Narahari, after he encountered Hinranyakashipu (Prahlada's father) and killed him. This is one of the most cherished hymns of the great holy text (7.9.11):

नैवात्मन: प्रभुरयं निजलाभपूर्णो
मानं जनादविदुष: करुणो वृणीते।
यद्यज्ञनो भगवते विदधीत मानं
तच्चात्मन: प्रतिमुखस्य यथा मुखश्री: ॥

You, the Lord of entire creation, are always all-fulfilled by virtue of your own nature and glory, and hence do not need any adoration, praise, or offering from anyone. Those who praise and make offerings to you do so out of their own ignorance. And you seem to accept all this solely because of your own mercy. Whatever praise, worship, or adoration is showered on you, all that conduces to the worshipper's own development, as is the case with the anointment done to the reflected face on oneself, whom the mirror reflects.

A question may arise as to why then so much worship of the Lord is done. Whatever the ignorant people do in the nature of adoration and offering brings about their own enrichment and elevation. By looking into an actual mirror we can see our face and decorate it, but what is done to the face in the mirror does not touch the mirror at all. Likewise, any praise, worship, or similar acts done to God verily enrich, empower, and elevate the worshipper himself, not God!

An impersonal, formless presence cannot be accessed by the ordinary human mind. At the same time, the mind wants to give vent to its feelings and affinity for the Lord. Hence the idol and various methods of worship are evolved. It is significant that at no time or place does the worshipper address the stone idol or the painted picture. Sitting before it, he thinks about, speaks to, and tries to interact with the Lord, the omnipresent. "O Lord, the omnipresent," is how the devotees think, speak, and address.

THE PRESENT WORK

Swamini Vanamali, the author of this book, is an ascetic who has been living in the Himalayan slopes in Rishikesh for many years. Hinduism always insists upon and exhorts people to take up austerity and asceticism as a natural culmination of spiritual life and pursuit. Generally the ascetic and the austere alone have lived the true spiritual life and disseminated spiritual wisdom in this holy land. True philosophers have always been ascetic and austere.

Naturally when someone like this speaks and writes about Sanatana Dharma, it will have an additional note of experiential vision and maturity. Such writing will always be distinct from the rest. Swamini Vanamali is not a new writer. Her earlier books are there to speak about her and her writing. Against the background of her earlier publications, this book on the science of the rishis has its distinct place and relevance. May this be well understood and the effort bring its destined fruition.

Society always will need enlightenment and hence the efforts toward this should be consistent in every generation. May Swamini Vanamali's effort have its distinct contribution and effectiveness in this direction.

My love, appreciation, and blessings for the author as well as her readers.

Antaraatma—the Inner Dweller, which is the Atman
Swami Bhoomananda Tirtha
Narayanashrama Tapovanam

Swami Bhoomananda Tirtha is a sannyasin belonging to the Tirtha lineage of Adi Sankaracharya. He is widely revered as a spiritual master and scholar and is particularly well versed in the *Bhagavad Gita*, the *Srimad Bhagavatam*, and the Upanishads. A social reformer, he is well known for his teachings on the application of Vedanta to the challenges of everyday life.

Bhutatmaaya Namaha!
Salutations to the Self in Every Creature!

INTRODUCTION

The Scientific Vision of the Rishis

After a study of some forty years and more of the great religions of the world, I find none so perfect, none so scientific, none so philosophic, and none so spiritual as the great religion known by the name of Hinduism. The more you know it, the more you will love it; the more you try to understand it, the more deeply you will value it.

ANNIE BESANT

Satyam eva jayati naanrutam.
Truth alone shall prevail, not falsehood.

MUNDAKA UPANISHAD

What is truth and how is it to be known? Time alone is the touchstone of truth. The universe exists on truth and anything that is not founded

1

on truth is automatically deleted by time. India has maintained the longest, unbroken continuity of civilization in the world. The ideas and beliefs of Hinduism—based on the eternal verities, *satyam, ahimsa,* and *dharma,* truth, nonviolence, and righteousness—have existed from time immemorial.

There was no antagonism between science and religion in India as there was in the West, since the religion is based on scientific truths. One ancient Hindu scripture, the *Ishavasya Upanishad,* says that there are two types of understanding, *vidya* and *avidya.* The interpretation given in the Upanishad is that *vidya* is eternal, experiential, spiritual knowledge or *para vidya,* while *avidya* is external, experimental, material knowledge or *apara vidya.* We should make use of the second to guide our lives so that we are led to the first. Unless both these types of knowledge are integrated into our lives, we will end up being blind or lame, as Einstein put it.

One who believes that science alone can take away all the miseries of life is like a blind man entering a dark room. However, one who believes that escaping the miseries of life can only be achieved by chanting mantras in the solitude of a cave is also entering blinding darkness. Hinduism has never held that blind faith can lead to liberation or that science alone can give you a utopian life. Both science and faith are necessary for a fulfilled life.

Most of the Westerners who came to India in the early part of the last century were totally incapable of appreciating the wonders of this ancient knowledge. This is because Hinduism is a most obscure and difficult religion to understand. What is generally exposed to the common eye is only the surface of a deep pond, which contains a treasure of gems that are not easily revealed to the cursory glance. Hinduism is as difficult for the uninitiated to understand as quantum physics for the layperson.

Actually, the word Hinduism is a misnomer. It was the name given by Westerners to those who lived below the Indus River. The actual name of Hinduism is Sanatana Dharma or "the way of eternal righteousness." This is the ancient law by which this cosmos has been created, sustained, and destroyed.

People have asked me how I dared to write about physics, which is an alien subject for me. My answer is that my in-depth knowledge of Hinduism has made it easy for me to understand quantum physics. The first time I read *The Tao of Physics* by Fritjof Capra, I was struck with wonder, for I instinctively understood what the physicist was trying to say. At the same time, many of the abstruse points in the *Bhagavad Gita* suddenly became crystal clear to me. Later, when I went through the Puranas (stories of gods written by the sage Vyasa), I was again struck at the amazing ways in which the great saints of the Puranas—Vyasa and Valmiki—had woven great scientific truths into their stories. These scientific truths are not what the ancient Western world believed to be true but the truths of the most modern kind— that of quantum physics.

One fact hit me like a sledgehammer—that right from the Vedas (the most ancient scriptures) to the Puranas, everything was completely scientific. For obvious reasons the sages did not expose this fact to the common eye. If we of the modern age, who are quite used to so many technical facilities, which we accept as commonplace, find it impossible to understand quantum physics, how much more would it have been impossible for people to understand what the sages were trying to say at a time when even things like ordinary matches were unheard of!

Sanatana Dharma is a living relic of the ancient past of not just India but the past of the whole history of humanity. Many of the forms of Hindu culture today are the same as they were more than ten thousand years ago. The ancient world never died in India. It still remains and can be contacted everywhere. The scientists of this culture were known as rishis. The credit for ensuring that this culture never died goes to them. They were both philosopher-saints and scientists and existed from the dawn of the Indian civilization, which is the dawn of time. The sages desired that humanity should progress materially as well as through a constant inner renewal of the cosmic law of righteousness, guided by the wisdom embedded in our scriptures.

What exactly is science? Science is something that tries to discover the different laws of nature. The ancient rishis who were the custodians of our culture were the greatest scientists ever known. There was nothing that they didn't know about Nature. She did not hide any of her abstruse wisdom from them. The rishis had extraordinary powers or *siddhis*. They could control the elements, travel with ease in the astral worlds, cover vast distances rapidly through the sky without any aircraft, catch sound and light waves in their minds and discern what was happening miles away. Their look could penetrate rocks and drill holes in metals, and they could have anything they wanted just by formulating a wish in their minds. No other civilization except the present one has reached such heights of knowledge as they had achieved.

Their knowledge of science in many fields, like mathematics, geometry, astrology, astronomy, and physics, was immense. Without the use of modern instrumentation, they were able to discover more things about this universe than what was discovered up to the nineteenth century by Western scientists. They knew that the earth went around the sun, that we are living in an expanding universe, and that matter is only energy in motion. They calculated the distance of stars and planets and could foretell the coming of the different comets. They even wrote predictions about the lives of people who would come after them. They could conjure up cities and palaces and wondrous meals and aerial vehicles even though they did not choose those things for their own lifestyle.

Unlike this culture that craves material wealth, they deemed that all knowledge of the external world was inferior knowledge and the highest knowledge was that of the true Self or Brahman. The experience of Brahman reveals the unity of life that underlies all living things. From this is born a tremendous love for all creatures and a deep desire to see human beings free themselves from the illusions and limitations in which they are involved. Love always wants to share what it gets and thus the rishis did everything in their power to unfold this Reality to the rest of humankind. They have opened our eyes to a world of mystery and beauty, not one of arid facts. If we could only behave in the way that they have taught us, we would certainly have made a heaven on earth. However, the rishis were aware of human limitations and sought methods to surmount them. As Reality can only be known by direct experience, they tried many types of methods called yogas in order to share this truth with the masses.

They were a special type of scientists, which we can call spiritual scientists. They realized that the foundation of the universe as well as of the human being is spiritual, not material. All the gross objects we see in the world actually have their source in the subtle, and not vice versa, as Western science would have us believe. Like Western scientists, the rishis also looked at the world and sought to find out the basic constituents of everything. However, unlike Western scientists, they realized that they would never find the meaning of anything in the world if they did not know the laws governing the functioning of their minds. So psychology—which is such a baby science in the West—was the first science that the rishis explored. They realized that the world existed because of the human mind and unless they learned to control the mind, they would never be able to find the meaning of anything in the universe, far less control it.

The intellect is the most powerful and versatile instrument known to us. Scientists make use of it to prize open the mysteries of the universe. It has led us to split the atom and reach the moon, but when it comes to discovering the truth of our innermost self, the intellect is confounded. It is capable of analyzing any object. It is a highly efficient instrument for objective study, but the rishis realized that it is sadly inadequate when it comes to subjective analysis.

When the Self itself becomes the object of study, the intellect is unable to surmount its inherent weakness and analyze itself. The Self is the torch that lights up the intellect, so how can it see itself? In other fields of investigation, the investigator is different from the object of investigation, but here the investigator is being investigated by himself! Sugar can never know the taste of tea. It can only dissolve in it and become one with it. The rishis devised a means by which the intellect could become so subtle that it could be dissolved. They found that in the state of deep meditation the intellect becomes so subtle that it dissolves like sugar into the object of investigation, which is the Self itself. Thus, the intellect's search for the Self ends in a glorious experience of the Divine rather than a comprehension of it.

The Divine of the Sanatana Dharma is a Universal Being or Paramatma, who transcends all boundaries of time, space, and causation. This Being is not bound to just the Hindus or even human beings but is available to the whole of creation. It has existed always and will continue to exist even if no one believes in It. It is the ultimate truth of everything and everyone. That being its foundation, Hinduism is the most tolerant religion in the world. As a goal-oriented religion, it offers us many paths of approach to God, which cater to different types of personalities. It does not insist that there is only one path and one way to approach the Paramatma or the Supreme. There are many paths and many ways.

Hinduism is accused of being pluralistic but pluralism means freedom—freedom of choice. It has no overall authority that dictates what every Hindu should or should not do. The first charter of human rights and liberties was given by Hinduism to every human being. The rishis have catered to every type of person. No one is cast out of the loving arms of this Divine Mother. Everyone is given freedom to worship god in his or her own way as suited to his or her own personality. We can take as many lives as we want but eventually every soul will be liberated. This is the beautifully consoling clarion call of Hinduism. Krishna tells Arjuna in the *Bhagavad Gita, Kaunteya pratijanihi, na me bhakta pranasyati*—"O Arjuna I give you my solemn promise that my devotee will never perish."

Anything that is static and stagnant will eventually decay and die. Just as water has to flow in order to keep itself free of impurities, so also a religion must have the ability to grow. Many of the highly evolved ancient religions of countries like Egypt and Mesopotamia have been wiped off the face of the earth with the passage of time, whereas

Hinduism has had the ability to evolve with the changing times. It can be compared to a banyan tree, which has spreading branches reaching out with ever more new shoots. That is why we find more religions within the Hindu faith than there are in the rest of the world put together. Though its fundamental concepts are ancient, it is capable of accepting and even welcoming all new ideas that are consistent with dharma or righteousness.

In keeping with the Vedic injunction that a guest should be treated with as much hospitality as one would treat a visiting divinity, Hinduism has always been gracious to the followers of other religions, and respectful of their gods, scriptures, and customs. The tolerance and openness of Hinduism has been historically unprecedented in the community of world religions and has been universally acclaimed. Unfortunately, in our headlong rush to devolve Hinduism of anything that might seem to even remotely resemble the closeminded sectarianism sometimes found in other religions, we tend to forget the obvious truth that Hinduism is itself a systematic and self-contained religious tradition in its own right. It is true that Hinduism is not an organized religion. It has no hierarchy of priests or popes or cardinals who impose orders that are obligatory on everyone.

However, like every other religion, Hinduism has a distinct and unique tradition, with its own built-in beliefs, worldview, traditions, rituals, concept of the Absolute, metaphysics, ethics, aesthetics, cosmology, cosmogony, and theology. The grand, systematic philosophical edifice that we call Hinduism today is the result of the extraordinary efforts and spiritual insights of the rishis, yogis, *acharyas,* and great gurus of our religion, guided by the transcendent light of the Vedic revelations, which has stood the test of time and withstood the onslaught and challenges of countless other cultures.

The time has come to allow the whole world to realize their inheritance, for the rishis did not intend the great secrets of the Vedas to be confined to India alone but wanted everything to be shared by all. In order to honor their desire, this book introduces the foundational texts, concepts, and profound insights bequeathed to us by the rishis, revealing their scientific knowledge, now being confirmed by the latest scientific discoveries, as well as conveying the depth and beauty of their transformative vision.

I conclude this introduction by offering my total and wholehearted prostrations at the feet of those rishis—Vasishta, Vishvamitra, and many others—who were the great gurus of our land as well as to the sages, Vyasa and Valmiki, who alone have inspired and given me the courage to write this book.

> *The Creator is perfect,*
> *He possesses perfect power,*
> *Whence is created perfect Nature.*
> *The perfect universe derives life*
> *From the perfect Creator.*
> *Let us comprehend this perfect power*
> *That bestows life on all beings.*
>
> ATHARVA VEDA

Loka Samasthath Sukhino Bhavantu!
Let the whole world be happy, healthy, and contented!

Shaswataaya Namaha!
Salutations to the Eternal!

1

The Rishis

Spiritual Scientists at the Dawn of Time

India is the cradle of the human race, the birthplace of human speech, the mother of history, the grandmother of legend, and the great-grandmother of tradition. Our most valuable and most constructive materials in the history of man are treasured in India only.

MARK TWAIN

From our Mother, the Dawn, may we be born as the seven seers, the original men of wisdom. May we become the sons of Heaven, the Angirasa seers. May we break open the mountain and illumine the Reality.

Just as our ancient and supreme Fathers, O sacred

*Fire, seeking the Truth, following the clear insight
sustaining the chant, broke through Heaven and Earth
and received the radiant Spirit.*

RIG VEDA 4.2.15–16

The rishis are the ones who gave us our heritage, our culture, and our way of life, known as the Sanatana Dharma. The word *rishi* is derived from an obscure Sanskrit root meaning "to see," for they were the seers or the hearers of the Vedic hymns that came from the mouth of Brahma. The word also designates "a singer of sacred hymns, an inspired poet or sage, any person who can invoke the deities in rhythmical speech or song of a sacred character." It might also have been derived from the Dravidian word *aric,* meaning "wise man, sage, astrologer, seer."

The four holy books known as the Vedas are considered to be *anadi* or "without beginning" and *apaurusheya* or "not the work of man." The modern mind, hemmed with notions of time and space, can hardly accept such statements. So Western scholars say that the rishis or sages wrote the Vedic hymns. However, the rishis would be the first to deny this statement. The rishis called themselves *mantra drashtas* or the "seers of the mantras," not the composers of the mantras. When we say that Newton discovered the law of gravity, it does not mean that he actually created it but that he brought an existing fact to the notice of the world. Likewise, the rishis cognized the mantras already in existence in etheric space and made them known to us. These mantras, like the laws of Nature, have always existed. As the rishis were the ones who brought the already existing mantras to our conscious knowledge, we always bow to their memory when repeating the mantras.

According to modern methods of calculating time, the Vedas must have been cognized by the rishis at the dawn of time, before the creation of language as we know it. At that time the world was still in its infancy, and the human being was only another animal, hunting for food and digging for roots and fruits. Those were the days when humans existed without proper food, clothing, or housing, and certainly not much of vocabulary. They had no names for the sun, moon, or any of the natural phenomena, even though they could see them. They were sitting, eating, talking, and so on, but had no names for any of these functions. In that inconceivable past, the divine knowledge of the Vedas was revealed to a set of superhuman beings with high receptivity, extraordinary memory, and an understanding far beyond that of even the most intelligent of modern human beings. Psychologists say that even a most intelligent human being like Einstein uses only 10 percent of his brain capacity, and the rest of us far less. From this we can guess that these beings were using 100 percent of their brain power. We can imagine that it was only with the revelation of the Vedas that the concept of communication was manifested in the world, by which the human being could not only converse with his fellow beings but also forge a link with posterity.

WHO WERE THE RISHIS?

Thousands of years have passed since this divine knowledge was first revealed to a small group of seers, traditionally named as Agni, Vayu, Aditya, and Angiras. Who exactly were these rishis? We know nothing about them but their names, but if we pause a moment to look at the amazing revelation of the Vedas, we will no doubt be struck with awe as to the nature of these seers. These spiritual giants lived in the Himalayas and strode across the Indo-Gangetic plains long before the dawn of historic time. They were the sublime expression of the perfect human being, the crown and cream of Nature's evolutionary cycle. These men were really suprahuman, multisensory beings who had the gift of inner vision and were able to see the past, present, and future as one huge canvas unrolling in front of them. They could go to the realms of the gods and demons, the demigods, and the titans of mythological lore and describe the events that went on at that time and even describe things that would take place at a future time.

Then came another group of rishis, or seers, with stupendous memory, who passed on this knowledge to successive generations. In India these great beings seem to have taken birth again and again in every age to keep up the Sanatana Dharma, which they cognized at the beginning of the world! It was indeed miraculous that in that misty morn of the universe there existed such beings that appeared to have attained the fulfillment of all human life, which has not been attained by the majority of humankind even in this age. This has led to the supposition that the rishis had an extraterrestrial origin. Considering the times in which they cognized the hymns, this is a very plausible theory.

These truly ancient beings had the power to choose the hour of their arrival and departure from this world. The compassion and love they bore to the land of their choice or origin is inexhaustible. It is only due to the power of their *tapasya* (austerity) that the world continues to retain its integrity. It is said that some of them, like Markandeya, continue to live in the eternal snows of the Himalayas, unseen by any human eye. These great souls are truly travelers in time who were born centuries ago yet have come to us to this very day, inviting us to go with them on their time travels. Even now they keep watch over us and look with compassion at us as we play with the toys of our ignorance.

Western historians have declared that the "authors" of the Vedas were an Aryan tribe that came across the Himalayas from the plateau of Asia Minor. This is known as the "Aryan invasion." The great German Indologist Max Muller was the first to think of this theory, which has no historical basis whatsoever. Indian historians have blindly accepted this concept and written it down in our history books; this is what is taught to Indian children today. How they came to form such a view is difficult to understand. The obvious place to get information about the rishis and the Vedic way of life is from the Vedas themselves. Nobody bothered to delve into this obvious source of information, perhaps because they were incapable of understanding it. But when we look into the Vedas, we see that there is no mention of such an invasion or exodus from Asia Minor across the mountains to the subcontinent of India. It is not possible that the Vedas would have neglected to mention such a stupendous venture.

According to the Vedas, the whole of the Vedic culture was developed along the banks of the great Sarasvati River, which was the great artery for the whole of north India, as the Ganga is today. However, Western historians claimed that the river was purely mythical. Why the rishis should have concocted such a fable of a mythical river is a mystery to anyone who reads the Vedas without prejudice. The Vedas clearly state all the geographical details of this river from its source to its end. It is only today that modern scientific research and satellite photos have verified the existence of this river, which was the very backbone of the Vedic scene and thus of the Hindu culture. Satellite pictures clearly show the river Sarasvati rising in the Himalayas and wending its way to the ocean. Remains of many settlements along the river have also been found. The river slowly dried up in 1900 BCE due to seismic movements and the gradual drying up of her tributaries, giving rise to the Thar Desert. Part of the river went underground and emerged in Allahabad, where it joined the other two great rivers of north India, the Ganga and the Yamuna. This highly spiritual spot is known as Triveni.

We can safely conclude that the Aryan invasion was a myth created by people with vested interests, who were anxious to prove that this amazing knowledge was an implant from outside. In fact, now it has been proven that Hinduism has existed since long before the great Harappan culture. The seals found in the Harappan valley have many of the Vedic signs on them like ॐ, the svastika, and the peepul tree.

The truth is that the holy land of India has produced countless amazing souls who are steeped in the divine essence and who can actually be called walking gods. They appeared in the remote past and continue to come even up to the present age.

Seven Sages

The *saptarishis* are the "seven sages" who are sent by Brahma—the Creator in the Hindu trinity—in every age or *manvantara* in order to uncover the wisdom of the Vedas from the etheric spheres. The rishis about whom we know belonged to the seventh manvantara or age, which is the present one, for which the patriarch is known as Vaivasvata Manu. The work of the rishis is to decode and make available to the ordinary, five-sensory mortal the great knowledge of creation, which they could hear through their inner ears. The *riks* (hymns of the Vedas) and the *samans* (melodies or chants) were the sounds that came to them through the etheric sphere and they memorized them perfectly.

In Hindu astronomy, the stars of the Big Dipper are named after the saptarishis. Metaphorically, they stand for the seven senses or the seven vital airs of the body. Their association with the stars gives more support to the theory that they might have been extraterrestrial beings. That is perhaps why we know very little of their lives, parents, or lineage. We know them only through their colossal revelations called the Vedas.

Many different lists of the names of the seven sages are given. Probably this differs from age to age. The rishis of the first manvantara are supposed to be Marichi, Atri, Angiras, Pulaha, Kratu, Pulastya, and Vasishta. There are other lists in the other manvantaras or eons. But most lists include Vasishta, Atri, Gautama, Bharadwaja, Vishvamitra, Jamadagni, Kashyapa, and Agastya.

The Rishis through the Ages

The chronological age of the first rishis is impossible to gauge. In Hinduism time is divided into four yugas or eons, which are cyclical and keep repeating endlessly. These yugas are known as Satya Yuga, Treta Yuga, Dwapara Yuga, and Kali Yuga. We are now living in the Kali Yuga. The lives of the rishis seem to have spanned across the first three yugas or eons. Thousands of years passed before the Satya Yuga gave place to the Treta Yuga and to Dwapara. However, to the rishis, time was a continuous river, so they passed from the Satya Yuga and entered the other yugas with ease, as if effortlessly floating on the cloud of time.

When we take a closer look at the Vedas in the next chapter, we will learn that the first portions of each are called the Samhitas (hymns). They are ecstatic tributes to natural creations, which are all supreme examples of the glory of the Divine, called *devas* or "the shining ones." The Samhita portion was obviously cognized when the rishis were living in the holy Himalayan Mountains. They lived in caves and derived their food from the ether and communed with the Divine. At that time it is possible that they did not have much to do with any other human beings, though it is obvious that they did communicate with each other. Perhaps this type of life existed for the whole of the Satya Yuga, when everything existed in truth (*satya*) alone. Perhaps at the end of this yuga they had gleaned as much as possible from the etheric sphere. They knew that the time was ripe to pass on this transcendental knowledge to the rest of humanity.

Therefore, they descended from the heights of the Himalayas and stepped into the great plain of north India. The next two portions of the Vedas, the Braahmanas and Aranyakas, were obviously authored and not cognized by the rishis as were the Samhitas. In these two portions the rishis did their best to inculcate the Vedic form of life, lived according to the high doctrines of the cosmic dharma. They established their modest *ashramas* or abodes all along the river. They married and had progeny to whom they taught the esoteric secrets of the Samhita portions. Many hamlets and soon towns and cities in which this type of communal living was taught grew up along the riverbanks.

During the next eon or yuga, known as Treta, some of the rishis left their ashramas and took up residence in the palaces of the kings. They knew that it was of utmost importance that those in power should follow the laws of dharma so that the land could flourish according to the ethical rules they had laid down. Moreover, only the kings had the power to conduct great *yajnas* (sacrifices) like the Somaveda,

Ashvamedha, Rajasuya, and so on, which were essential to the well-being of the land. The rishis taught the kings all the esoteric secrets of government, weaponry, and the art of ruling. Some of them were even given the great nuclear weapon known as the Brahmastra. But this was an esoteric secret given only to those who were morally capable of using it at the right time for the good of the world and not for personal gratification. To the farmers the rishis gave the knowledge of agriculture, while many secrets of medicinal plants were imparted to the physicians.

Lord Rama was one of the great kings of the Treta Yuga. The guru of his dynasty—the solar race—was the famous rishi Vasishta. To Rama he not only imparted the esoteric secrets of statecraft but also the great message of the Upanishads known as the *Yoga Vasishta,* by mastering which Rama became a truly evolved soul.

This yuga gave way to the next called Dwapara. Here again we meet the rishis and realize how much they must have affected and influenced life both in the courts and elsewhere. All the vast scientific knowledge they had amassed was passed on to the people of the land. That is why India had such a glorious civilization while Europeans were still living like barbarians.

This must have come as a shock to the first Westerners who came to India! So they took great pains to suppress this fact. They declared that India had no historical records and whatever was said in the Vedas and Puranas was pure invention, with no basis in fact. In one fell swoop our glorious culture was declared to be myth and fable! Unfortunately, Indian historians aped all this nonsense. The fact is that the early Western historians had vested interests and knew that the only way to impose their religion on the Indians was to belittle their culture and cast scorn on their gods. So the rishis have also chosen to incarnate themselves in this Kali Yuga—the age of decadence—in order to preserve the eternal dharma.

Apart from the four Vedas (*Rig Veda, Sama Veda, Yajur Veda,* and *Atharva Veda*), the principles of Hindu dharma are to be found in the texts of ten other disciplines. These are the six Vedangas, or auxiliaries to the Vedas—Shiksha, which teaches the correct pronunciation of the Vedic hymns, Vyakarna or grammar, Chandas or meter, Nirukta or etymology, Jyotisha or astronomy, and Kalpa or procedure. To these are added Mimamsa, the interpretation of the Vedic texts, Nyaya or logic, Purana or mythology, and the Dharma Shastras, which contain codes of conduct for all human beings. All knowledge and wisdom are enshrined in these fourteen fields. Normally four more books are added to these, which are known as Upangas or appendices to the Vedangas. They are Ayurveda, the science of life and health, Arthashastra, the science of wealth or economics, Dhanur Veda, the science of weapons, missiles, and warfare, and Gaandharva Veda, or treatises on fine arts like music, art, dance, drama, sculpture, and so on. The Vedangas and the Upangas are all derived from the Vedas and should be studied along with the Vedas so that their meaning becomes clearer.

LIVING IN BRAHMAN

A *brahmarishi* is one who is constantly in communion with Brahman, the Supreme Godhead. That is to say, these rishis are always in a state of cosmic consciousness in which they are immediately in touch with everything in the cosmos. They can be called the highest class of rishis, who have attained the divine knowledge (*brahmajnana*) or unity with Brahman. This knowledge of the Supreme is attained after years of austerity, meditation, study, and selfless service to the Supreme, resulting in total self-purification. It is a combination of physical, mental, and spiritual exertion. In the Vedas, a rishi is strictly defined as one to whom the Vedic hymns were originally revealed. They are the ones who have *mantra drashta* or the ability to "see" the mantras. Other sages can never be called rishis, *maharishis,* or brahmarishis, whatever their merits. Since the order was created by Lord Brahma, it is impossible for Hindu priests and scholars, or contemporary saints, to anoint rishis, maharishis, or brahmarishis, although many persons use such epithets for themselves or for their gurus.

Actually the Vedic term for the saptarishis was *braahmanas,* since they were the ones who were created by Brahma and knew Brahman. They came to be known as *brahmarishis* later, during the post Vedic period when the term *braahmana* came to be used for a person who was born in the brahmin caste, which meant that they were born in the *gotra* or clan of one of these brahmarishis. Thus, we find another list of saptarishis who are also *gotra pravartakas,* that is, founders of the brahmanical clans. This second list appeared at a later period in history, but they are still very ancient. It is an amazing thing that these families have existed to the present age. Hence, the present-day brahmins or braahmanas claim to have an unbroken lineage coming down from the Vedic rishis of more than ten thousand years ago. To this very day all brahmins claim to have been born in the gotra of one of these incredibly ancient sages, such as Vasishta. This is another unique feature of Hindu culture. No other culture can claim to have people who can trace their lineage to such antiquity.

Let us take a peep into the life of these great beings. Nature itself was only a backdrop for their minds. Everything that happens, happens within the mind. During the early hours of the morning and when the sun was at its zenith and again when it set in the western sky, the rishis would sit for meditation. These are the times of the day known as *sandhyas,* when the sun's rays have the greatest power to evoke thoughts of the Supreme in the minds of mortals. They are particularly conducive for meditation. At these times the rishis could most clearly cognize the divine hymns, feeling them as vibrations in their hearts.

Even at other times, when they walked around, they were in the superconscious state known as *samadhi.* They did not have to work for their living since they needed nothing and were dependent on nothing. They gleaned their sustenance from the ether. They looked at everything but saw only Brahman. That alone pervaded everything. They were one with That and therefore they did not exist as separate personalities. Only That One existed. That Supreme Truth, which manifests itself all the time in everything, is an eternal, infinite, and absolute self-existence, self-awareness, and self-delight—*sat-chit-ananda*. It supports and pervades all things. It is present in the human being as the *atman*. It is not only the Absolute but also the omnipresent reality in which all that is relative exists as Its forms and movements.

Having submerged themselves in the ocean of existence, consciousness, and bliss, they had no trace of ego, even though they existed in a human body. They can be known only through their words in the Vedas. They have left nothing else. They left no chronicle of their achievements or images that might have survived the course of time.

All forms in the physical world are created by the Supreme Consciousness through the shaping of light. The rishis who lived immersed in the Pure Consciousness of Brahman were quite capable of conjuring up any form they chose through the medium of light. This was a natural thing for them. But even though they could materialize anything they wished, they did not seek to carve in stone or wood or make effigies or temples or in any way try to immortalize themselves in this world even though they were perfectly competent to do so. They knew that this world was only as real as the morning mist and would melt with the rising of the sun. The sun of their consciousness was at its zenith and they did not desire the trifles of the world. They have taught us the truth that we will not gain universality unless we are prepared to lose our individuality.

These rishis had no desires. They were quite happy with the forms that existed in the world, which had been fashioned by that Supreme Consciousness. They were content with whatever Nature provided. They did not yearn to possess more for the simple reason that they possessed the wish-fulfilling cow of plenty in their own minds, which was capable of granting every desire they had. Having found the secret of all existence, they continued to live only with the one desire, *lokasamgraham*—"the good of the world." They were the embodiments of compassion.

They chose to live their lives in little hermitages or ashramas situated in the middle of jungles, where wild animals roamed unafraid.

Every day was a new day. They never stored or hoarded for the next day. The only thing they tended very carefully was fire or *agni*. Into that fire they poured their oblations to the gods. They kept a few cows, which supplied the butter and ghee necessary for these oblations. They cultivated the land only to the extent that they needed. They were the very embodiments of simplicity and contentment. They desired nothing from the world, for they had found the source of all happiness within themselves. Therefore, they could not be tempted by the baubles of a world that they knew to be ephemeral.

They needed no commandments to keep them to the right path, for they were the very embodiments of dharma, or the cosmic order. They have given humanity the idea of what dharma, or cosmic law, means through the example of their own lives. They did not wish to conquer or control, even though they had the power to control the whole world. They were conscious of their inner power and so they were unafraid of anyone or anything. Actually all of us possess this inner power but we do not know it and thus we think we have to depend on external powers to protect us. We are riddled with fears and we try to protect ourselves by maintaining police forces and accumulating weapons and armies.

Their amazing experience could not be communicated in ordinary language so they taught their disciples in the form of questions and answers. These dialogues are recorded in what are known as the Upanishads, which come at the end of every Veda. The Upanishads use terse and concise language to point out Reality. However, unlike the world of Western science, which is open only to a few intellectuals, the magic world of the rishis has benefited even the uneducated and children. They have shown us that if heaven exists, it has to be made on this very earth.

> *In the beginning was the golden womb (Hiranyagarbha),*
> *The seed of elemental existence,*
> *The only Lord of all that was born,*

He upheld the heaven and earth together,
To what God other than him should we dedicate our life?

ATHARVA VEDA 4.2.7

I am rta, the truth. I was born in the beginning of
creation before the birth of the gods. The rishis call me
amrita.

SAMA VEDA 5.9.4

I am satya, the truth. I manifest myself in the great epic.
I appear as the truth through the jataveda fire. None is
above me. I am the Ultimate.

ATHARVA VEDA 1.1.5

Loka Samasthath Sukhino Bhavantu!

Vishvakarmaaya Namaha!
Salutations to the Maker of All Things!

2

The Vedas

Royal Road to Knowledge

*In the great teaching of the Vedas, there is no touch of
sectarianism. It is of all ages, climes and nationalities,
and is the royal road for the attainment of the Great
Knowledge.*

THOREAU

*India was the motherland of our race and Sanskrit the
mother of Europe's languages. India was the mother of
our philosophy and much of our mathematics, of the
ideals embodied in Christianity, of self government and
democracy. In many ways Mother India is the mother of
us all.*

WILL DURANT (AMERICAN HISTORIAN 1885–1981)

The two primary factors that distinguish the individual uniqueness of the great world religious traditions are: the scriptural authority upon which the tradition is based and the fundamental religious tenets that it espouses. Thus a Jew, for example, can be understood as someone who accepts the Torah as his scriptural guide and believes in the monotheistic concept of God espoused in those scriptures. A Christian can be understood as a person who accepts the Gospels as his scriptural guide and believes that Jesus is the only son of God who incarnated himself in order to save humankind from its sins. Similarly, a Muslim is someone who accepts the Quran as his scriptural guide and believes that there is no God but Allah and that Mohammed is his only prophet.

The determination of being a follower based on accepting and attempting to live by a religion's scriptural authority is no less true of Hinduism. By definition, a Hindu is an individual who accepts the Vedas as the authoritative guide to his religion, and who strives to live in accordance with dharma, God's divine laws as revealed in the Vedas and explained in easy language in the Puranas. In keeping with this standard definition, the great exponents of the six traditional schools of Hindu philosophy (*shad darshanas*) insisted on the acceptance of the scriptural authority (*shabda pramana*) of the Vedas as the primary criterion for distinguishing a Hindu from a non-Hindu, as well as distinguishing Hindu philosophical positions from non-Hindu ones. The historical standard for being a Hindu has been acceptance of the Vedas (meaning the complete canon of the Vedic scriptures, such as the four Vedas, the Upanishads, and the *Bhagavad Gita,* the *Mahabharata* and *Ramayana* epics, the Puranas, and so on) as the scriptural authority, and living in accordance with the dharmic principles as embedded in these scriptures. Thus, any Indian who rejects the authority of the Veda is obviously not a Hindu—regardless of their birth. On the other hand, an American, Canadian, Russian, Brazilian, Indonesian, or Indian who accepts the authority of the Veda obviously is a Hindu, not by race, but by commitment.

The Vedas are the sacred heritage not only of India but of all humanity. However, until recently, translations and interpretations of these sacred books have been made by Western historians and scholars who had little or no concept of such lofty ideals and ideas. Our own Indian historians blindly copied what was said by the Westerners and therefore this great heritage of divine knowledge has been obscured.

THE AGE OF THE VEDAS

All other religions have been able to fix a date for their sacred books. The teachings of the Buddha can be dated to 500 BCE when the Buddha lived. There is no argument about the date of the New Testament, which was 2,000 years ago. Everyone agrees that the Quran was enscribed 1,200 years ago. But so far no one has been able to fix the age of the Vedas. This is because of the unique way in which the Vedas have come down to us. They were first heard by some great rishis who imparted them orally to their disciples. Then the knowledge was handed down orally through the ages, only being written down much later.

It is a fundamental belief of the Sanatana Dharma that the Vedas are sanatana (eternal) and apaurusheya (not composed by any human being). However, most Westerners and Western-educated Indians cannot accept the fact that the Vedas are without beginning. Much time and money have been spent on research on this subject and people have fixed the time of their composition at 6000 BCE, since certain planetary positions mentioned in the Vedas took place at that time. While it is easy to fix dates by planetary positions for cultures that have existed only for a few centuries, this is not possible for cultures that have existed for millennia, for the same type of planetary position could have existed many times within the course of that length of time. Therefore, such calculations cannot be used to calculate the age of the Vedas.

Another method used in attempts to determine the age of the Vedas is to examine the language used. All the scripts used in India today owe their origin to what is called the Braahmi script. Of course, in the case of edicts engraved by kings on metal and stone, this would be a great help to confirm their age. However, the Vedas were never at any time engraved on metal or stone, so how could their age be determined by the script?

Still another method of determining age is by the style of talking. Spoken languages change tremendously over time. For example, the original Anglo-Saxon language, which is less than a thousand years old, cannot be easily understood by the modern Englishman. But the Vedic language is not a spoken language, even though the Vedas are chanted every day in all parts of India. So this method cannot be used with the Vedas, since they are still being chanted as they were from the dawn of time. The reason why the Vedic sounds have been maintained in their pristine purity is because the desired effect can be produced only by the correct intonation of the mantras. The rishis took great pains to see that the sounds would not suffer any mutations as words in everyday use.

The vast amount of knowledge in the Vedas was compiled into the four books known as *Rig Veda, Yajur Veda, Sama Veda,* and *Atharva Veda* by the great sage Vyasa. Because of the invaluable work he did, he has been called Veda Vyasa, and he is regarded as Hinduism's first guru. Each of the four divisions was given to one of his disciples to memorize, since with the passage of time there was no one who was capable of memorizing all four Vedas. Thus each Veda has come to be associated with the disciple through whom it has come down to us.

In their thirst for dating everything, modern Western researchers declare the *Rig Veda* to be the oldest, whereas our *shastras* (scriptures) say that all four Vedas are without beginning, available to the world from the dawn of creation. The *Rig Veda* itself contains references to the *Yajur* and *Sama Vedas.* So how can some be labeled as earlier and some later? All the dates and periods attributed to the Vedas by Western scholars are an attempt to ridicule the sacred and eternal heritage of India. In fact, the Vedas reckon time as existing before the time of our current universe, so how can we fix their age?

THE BREATH OF BRAHMAN

At the beginning of every cosmic cycle, Paramatma (the Absolute) breathes the divine words into the mind of Brahma (the Creator) and these sound vibrations result in the creation of the world. Later, through divine grace, certain rishis hear these words known as *shruti* (that which is heard). The crown and glory of the human race, these rishis were fit to receive and impart the words of the Supreme to enlighten human beings so that we might live happily in this world and become aware of our innate divinity.

If the rishis were not the authors of the Vedas, can we then conclude that God created them? This is also not true because in Hinduism, we do not believe that God created the world one fine day. Creation is seen as cyclical and not linear as in Western theology. One creation or *shrishti* is followed by a *laya* or dissolution, after which another creation or shrishti takes place. This is an endless process. At the end of every Brahma's cosmic period, the Vedic knowledge in its gross form disappears, only to reappear in Brahma's next cycle of creation.

Brahman, the one eternal and unchanging Being, has existed always. It is the time continuum from which the universe of matter appears and disappears from time to time. The Veda itself says that the Vedas are the very breath of Brahman (Paramatma or the Supreme Self). Just as our breath is an essential part of us, the Vedas are an essential part of Brahman; as Brahman has always existed, so have the Vedas. That is why they are termed *anadi* or without beginning.

Modern science defines sound as vibration. The rishis became aware of the cosmic breath in the form of vibrations, due to their *tapas* or austerity. Just as electromagnetic waves are converted into sonic waves, which can be captured and heard by us via a radio or TV, the cosmic vibrations became audible to the rishis who used only their internal apparatus. They decoded them and gave them to all humanity in the form of the Vedic mantras. Just as some type of life-giving serums are preserved with greatest care in laboratories, so the rishis took infinite pains to see that the Veda mantras, which are for universal benefit, were preserved without resort to writing.

The Vedas were passed from generation to generation in the ancient method of learning by listening, in the master-disciple tradition. Why were the Vedas not written down? The first reason is that writing was unknown at the time when the Vedas were arranged by Veda Vyasa. Another equally and perhaps more important reason is that some sounds do not lend themselves to be accurately reproduced phonetically. To get a desired station on the TV or radio, perfect tuning is necessary. So it is with the Vedic mantras. The svara or pitch and amplitude of sound should be perfect. Just as a small change in wavelength brings us a different TV station, so also any change in the chanting of a Vedic mantra produces a different effect. It is because of this that it has been stipulated that the Vedas should only be learned by ear from a competent guru. The Vedanga called *siksha* provides guidance for perfect pronunciation.

The Vedic seers were experts in phonetics who knew that the Vedic mantras had extraordinary powers. When they are chanted with the correct intonation the sound of the mantras activates our nerve centers and affects the atmosphere, resulting in individual as well as collective well-being. Collective does not refer only to humanity. No other religious text emphasizes the well-being of the animal and plant world as much as the Vedas, which say, "Let four-legged and two-legged creatures prosper"—*sham no astu dvipade sham chaturpade*. The same verse goes on to pray for the well-being of shrubs, trees, mountains, and rivers—in fact the whole of creation.

Modern research has demonstrated the effect of music on the growth of plants—increasing yields, and so on. Similarly, the outstanding feature of the Vedas lies in the fact that, apart from the actual meaning of the words, the sound of the mantras has great effect, so listening to them will give us great benefit even if we do not understand the meaning.

The science of phonetics, so recent in the West, was highly

advanced in Vedic times. There are many sounds in the Veda that fall in between two syllables. These can only be transmitted orally. Moreover, the Vedic mantras have to be recited in a certain specified rhythm to produce the correct vibrations. Some sounds have to be in a high chromatic scale, some medium, and others low. However much we try to aid the pronunciation by text notations, improper accent, intonation, and pronunciation can all creep in. This leads to a lessening of the intended effect or can even produce an opposite effect. It is easy to imagine the different impact on us of a sound produced in a high or low pitch. Our emotional response and even the cosmic forces that regulate the orderliness of Nature change with the differences in intonation.

Knowing the Vedas to be of supreme importance and a perfect treasurehouse of inexhaustible and infallible wisdom, the rishis took infinite pains to ensure that the purity and perfection of the sound and vibrations were preserved for posterity. In order to do this, they created a caste called the brahmins (knowers of Brahman), whose only duty was to memorize and pass on this knowledge to the future generations. They were the custodians of this supreme wisdom and the kings had the responsibility of seeing to their welfare. This had both a good and bad side. It certainly ensured the purity of the knowledge and even today the Vedas are recited exactly as they were recited ten thousand years ago; this is a remarkable phenomenon and would never have taken place had the brahmin caste not been created. In a similar way, the Jews have designated rabbis for the purpose of preserving their scriptures. In Israel, for example, the rabbis and those who take to a religious life are exempt from military duty and other governmental duties, just as the ancient brahmins were. However, the creation of a special caste had the disadvantage of making the Veda unavailable to the common people.

Most of the research on the Vedas has been done by Westerners who have unearthed much of our ancient wisdom and have been struck by its greatness. In fact, we owe a lot to these Westerners who have

taken the trouble to find out some of our ancient scripts and preserve them. However, they did not realize that the essential purpose
of the Vedas was to ensure the well-being of the whole universe, not
just of human beings, by spreading the sound of the Vedic mantras
and encouraging the performance of the Vedic rites. The Veda, which
is a living force intended for the betterment of the universe, has been
decoded and incarcerated into voluminous tomes to lie idle on library
shelves!

In addition to being without a beginning the Vedas also claim to
be endless. Actually the Vedas are a vast ocean of endless knowledge.
What has come to us is only a portion, which was revealed to the rishis.
As mentioned, the Vedas are the breath of Brahman or Paramatma.
The vibrations caused by that breath always exist in space, through all
the destructive deluges that have taken place from time to time in the
universe. Those vibrations have no decay or death and are always available to those who are attuned to them.

THE ONE AND THE MANY ARE THE SAME

The Vedas taught worship of the gods of Nature, such as the sun, sky,
wind, and fire, but they emphasized the fact that behind the facade of
these many gods, there is but one Supreme God. The Veda talks of that
Paramatma or Supreme Soul as manifesting itself through the various
divinities. This concept was originally expressed in the *Rig Veda* itself:

Ekam sat vipra bahudha vadanti.
Only One exists; sages call it by various names.

Vedic theism is pure and simple and is a most natural monotheism
invoking the One mighty force behind all forces and the divine light
behind all effulgences. The existence of the Supreme Reality in the cosmos can be realized by the purposeful dynamism of the Lord's creation.
Hence, the Vedic verses worship the Lord by invoking Nature's bounties

known as devas. The hymns of the Vedas invoke the Supreme Being who is the sole master of creation. This Supreme Reality is not merely an abstract philosophical concept but a dynamic reality, which we have to invoke every minute for our personal fulfillment. Vedic theism is a vibrant concept. Even though we might not know the Supreme, even though we might deny It, the fact is that It is intimately connected with us at every moment. We might forget It, we might ignore It, but It will not neglect us. That Supreme, though unmanifest, is manifested through Its divine manifestations. It is the effulgence of the sun; It is the mighty force behind Nature; It is the light of all lights, terror of all terrors, sweetness of everything that is sweet, and the actor behind every activity. The Vedas try to contact It through Its creation.

In Vedic poetry our tiny self and the Supreme Self are described as two birds that are mutual friends and companions and who live on the same branch of a tree. The *jivatma* or the embodied soul tastes the fruits of the tree (of life). When they are sweet, the jivatma rejoices; when they are sour or bitter, it feels despondent and sad. The Paramatma or Supreme Lord (the other bird on the same tree) watches the joys and sorrows of Its companion with compassion but will not interfere. When the first bird is replete with all the sense pleasures offered by the world, it loses its taste for sensual pleasures and turns toward the other bird, which has been its constant companion, realizing that in the Supreme lies joy without sorrow and love without any expectation of return.

The hymns of the Vedas are grouped into worship offered to the different devas such as Agni, Indra, Varuna, Soma, Rudra, and so on, representing the various powers and attributes of the Divine. The Vedas have definitely stated that these devas are only aspects of the One Supreme. The importance given to these devas can be understood only when one sees the same Supreme Divinity behind the splendor of all Its manifestations in Nature.

Although the four Vedas may appear to be different in some aspects like the method of recitation, all of them have a common goal—to ensure the well-being of the universe and to help everyone toward spiritual progress. Another singular feature of all the Vedas is that none of them say, "This is the only way," and "this is the only God." They all say that any path followed with faith and devotion to any deva will lead to the same goal since the goal is one. No other holy book in any other religion advocates the pursuit of different paths. Every religion insists that only its own doctrine will lead to salvation. The Vedas alone have such a breadth of vision that all four of them say that the same truth can be realized in many ways, since truth is One and the same for all!

STRUCTURE OF THE VEDAS

The Vedic hymns can be grouped into six types—hymns on creation, devotional hymns, hymns on revelation, hymns for certain types of action, hymns on the splendor of the Lord, and hymns on the positive sciences.

Each of the four Vedas—*Rig, Yajur, Sama,* and *Atharva*—has four portions, known as the Samhitas, Braahmanas, Aranyakas, and Upanishads. Generally, when we speak of mastering the Vedas, we mean only the mastering of the Samhita portion. This is because the Samhitas are the foundation of each Shaakha or branch; these are the hymns that were seen or heard by the rishis.

Rig Veda

The *Rig Veda* appears in the form of riks or "hymns of praise" to the various deities. It contains an astonishing stock of 35,000 words in 10,170 verses (mantras or riks), which have the intrinsic potentiality for coining new words. The most astonishing thing about this is that these verses were chanted by the rishis at a time when language as we know it did not exist. Since the *Rig Veda* talks of Agni both at the beginning and at the end, it has been mistakenly said to advocate only the worship of Agni. Actually Agni or fire should be taken to mean the light of the soul or consciousness (*atma chaitanya*)—the glow of the soul's awakening. The final *sukta* (hymn) of the *Rig Veda* says:

Let all meet and think as with one mind. Let all hearts unite in love. Let the goal be common. May all live in happiness with a common purpose!

Yajur Veda

The word *yajus* is derived from the root *yaj,* which means "worship" or "sacrifice." The word *yajna* is also derived from it. The chief purpose of the *Yajur Veda* is to show us how to use the mantras in the *Rig Veda* in a practical way in the yajnas or sacrificial rituals. Almost all the mantras in the form of hymns in the *Rig Veda* are also to be found in the *Yajur Veda*. In addition, it describes in prose the details for the performance of the different yajnas. While *Sama Veda* teaches us how to chant the hymns in a poetic way, *Yajur Veda* teaches us the actual performance of the yajnas using these hymns and mantras. There are two branches of the *Yajur Veda,* known as *shukla* (white) and *krishna* (black).

If we want to perform any of the great yajnas of the Vedas, we have to go the *Yajur Veda.* Many great yajnas, such as Somayaga, Vaajapeya, Rajasuya, Ashvamedha, and many others, are found only in this Veda. It also contains some mantras and hymns not found in the *Rig Veda.* The most famous of these is the Sri Rudram or the hymn in praise of Lord Shiva.

Sama Veda

Sama means *shanti* or "peace." In the *Sama Veda,* many of the hymns of the *Rig Veda* are set to music. Sama Gaana or the music of the *Sama Veda* can be said to be the basis and source of the seven notes that are fundamental to all music, the source from which both the Hindustani music of the north and the Carnatic music of the south derived its inspiration. It is said that all the gods can be propitiated by singing the Sama hymns. In all yajnas one of the priests has to chant the *Sama Veda* in order to keep the gods happy. Thus in the *Bhagavad Gita,* Lord Krishna proclaims that among the Vedas, he is *Sama Veda.* In the *Lalita Sahasranaama,* or the Thousand and One Names of Lalita, the Divine Mother is said to be Samagaana Priya—one who loves the music of the *Sama Veda.*

Atharva Veda

Atharva was the name of a great rishi, who was the one to bring the hymns of the *Atharva Veda* to our knowledge. The Atharva mantras are in prose as well as in verse. In this Veda many esoteric secrets as well as cures for various ailments are revealed. The mantras are meant to ward off evil, bestow perfect health, destroy enemies, and so on. It also has hymns to some devas that are not mentioned in the other three Vedas. It has a famous hymn to Nature called Prithvi Suktam. Book 11 of this Veda has a hymn devoted to every little thing concerning the human body, starting from the outer covering to the innermost complex. Countless hymns report on medicines and cures for a number of diseases. The *Atharva Veda* is actually a storehouse of esoteric secrets on health but very little of this is available to us now.

Many sciences found in this Veda were discovered by the modern world many centuries later. Physics, chemistry, geology, medicine, astronomy, astrology, and so on are all discussed. It has a lot of information on filtration, solution, crystallization, distillation, and sublimation, all of which were used for medical purposes. Everything concerning what are now known as oxides of copper, iron, and zinc, and sulphates of iron, copper, gold amalgam, and white lead, and how to make dyes with a variety of vegetable products were fully dealt with.

What is most important about these scientific facts given in all the Vedas is that science was not merely a theoretical subject found only in laboratories. It was a living, throbbing study, which found its utility in all aspects of human life, leading to a fuller and happier life for humans, animals, and plants. Chemistry was used to help find medical remedies. Astrology also had a definite bearing on chemistry and medicine, since the planets—sun, moon, Saturn, Jupiter, Mars, Venus, and Mercury—were associated with different metals used in gem therapy like gold, silver, lead, tin, iron, copper, and mercury. Many references to this are given in this Veda.

Vedic mathematics is now seen to be of a superior quality. Consecutivity of numbers from 1 to 10 is found in the eleventh book of the *Atharva Veda,* addition of numbers with multiples of 10 in the fifth book, and multiplication by 11 in the nineteenth book. Notation by decimal value was well known in India even from those ancient times.

Unfortunately, this Veda, which was once prevalent in north India, seems to have vanished from most areas. Even in south India there are no pure Atharva Vedins left. A few families of Atharva Vedins can still be found in Gujarat, Saurashtra, and Nepal. But from the few mantras and hymns of this Veda that are available to us now, we can understand that this Veda is a veritable storehouse of scientific information. Unfortunately no one in this modern world has the enormous spiritual and intellectual capacity capable of capturing these vibrations.

The Interplay of Action and Wisdom

While the mantras or hymns of the Samhitas are the most important part of the Vedas, each of the other portions has an important role. The Braahmanas act as a guide to explain how each of the mantras should be understood. They also explain how the Vedic rituals or yajnas are to be performed. Aranyaka is derived from the word aaranya or forest. According to the Aranyakas, it is important to understand the reasons why yajnas are to be performed.

Yajnas and other rituals are prescribed for those who live in homes and lead the life of a householder. But it must be understood that Vedic rituals are intended not only for material benefits but also for mental purity. Only those who have attained mental purity should take to the solitude of the forests for further concentration and meditation. All other practices are only a preparation for the ultimate goal of life, which is to meditate and find out the true nature of the Self.

The Braahmanas and the Aranyakas contain a vast amount of scientific knowledge, which has only been discovered in very recent times by the modern world. As has been mentioned, chemistry, physics, geometry, mathematics, astronomy, astrology, botany, geology, anatomy, and medicine are fully dealt with in these two portions of the Vedas. All the arts were touched upon, as well as agriculture, architecture, and transportation. Ample advice is given in these portions to enable human beings to live long, healthy, and happy lives, profitable both to themselves and to the world.

The Upanishads contain the ultimate message and purpose of the Vedas. They are therefore known as Vedanta—firstly because they are placed at the end of the Vedas, coming after the Aranyakas, and secondly because they are the goal or end to which the Veda points.

The Vedas thus recognize the existence of two worlds and give methods by which both can be satisfied. The difference between modern science and Vedic science is that modern science totally ignores the existence of another world in which the dualities of this world do not exist. The Vedas, on the other hand, always understood this. The instructions for leading a good and dharmic life given in the Braahmana and Aranyaka portions of the Veda, together called *karma kanda* (portion pertaining to action), are the preparation for understanding the *jnana kanda* (portion pertaining to wisdom), the Upanishads, which deal with the transcendental reality.

At times the karma kanda and the jnana kanda of the Vedas have been interpreted as being at variance with each other. In order to understand this apparent discrepancy, we have to understand what life is about. Even though the rishis realized that the goal of life was to discover the Self within and establish oneself in that unity, they also realized that for most people duality alone was real and unity just a dream. The Vedas say *brahma satyam jagat mithya*—"Brahman alone is real and the world an illusion"—yet the rishis were fully conscious of the fact that for the majority of humans the reverse is true. In their compassion they did not want to reject anyone; thus the second part of the Vedas teaches all the rituals by following which one can have a good and auspicious life in the world.

Modern science also gives us many techniques and devices by which we can live in comfort and affluence, but it considers the human being, Nature, and God to be totally disconnected. That has led to a lifestyle achieved at the cost of defiling Nature and plundering her resources. Many of the modern innovations do not take into consideration the fact that Nature is actually a living entity, throbbing with life; we think nothing of wresting from her whatever we want. This is what has led to the unhappiness that we suffer despite the fact that we have more gadgets and so-called materialistic comforts than any generation preceding us.

The method of the rishis was quite different. They wooed the devas or the subtle beneficial forces of Nature and maintained their balance. This brought prosperity to humankind as well as to animals and plants. As long as we think the world to be real, we have to propitiate these devas so that we can continue to live in comfort and prosperity. This is what the karma kanda guides us to do.

The scientific and other knowledge detailed in the karma kanda is known as *apara vidya,* or that knowledge that is verifiable through experiments. But, as has been pointed out, the inner essence of the Vedas always directs us toward the unity of life, the discovery of which is the goal of life. That was called *para vidya,* or Supreme Knowledge, which is verifiable only through personal experience. The jnana kanda portion of the Vedas gives us that Supreme Knowledge by knowing which everything else is automatically known.

The Braahmanas deal with the world as seen by classical physics whereas the Upanishads deal with the quantum world. When the latter becomes a matter of actual experience, the so-called real world experienced by the majority of humanity is seen to be an illusion, which modern-day quantum physicists have found to their astonishment.

With the dawn of this quantum age, scientists have even begun to think that there may be something called a life current flowing through the universe, variously referred to by religions as the Divine Consciousness or God or Brahman or other terms. They are trying to give proof for what humankind has had faith in, but no solid evidence for, from the dawn of time. Scientists have proved in the laboratory that the dualistic world that we think we can see is a myth, a shadow cast on the wall. The only reality is that higher collective consciousness, which exists for all time and in all places. You may call it God or whatever else you choose to call it. The Vedas called it Brahman.

YAJNAS AND THE ENERGY FIELD

The most important of the Vedic rituals is known as yajna, "worship" or "sacrifice." Yajna involves the performance of certain prescribed rituals with the aid of Agni (the god, Fire). The Vedas describe small and big yajnas that can be done by human beings. There is also reference to the cosmic yajna, which goes on incessantly in Nature, producing sunshine, clouds, rainfall, vegetation, and the different natural cycles.

The fire yajnas were conducted in huge open-air enclosures known as *yajna shalaas,* and they were really the very first scientific laboratories. Here the sages examined the flora and fauna of the land, surveyed organic and inorganic resources, and laid the foundations of a welfare state. The domestication of animals, the science and craft of agriculture, and the utilization of all types of resources for food, clothing, and housing were some of the earliest undertakings of the Vedic age. They praised Nature, the universal mother, with lovely hymns. They did not defile or desecrate her or assume that her riches belonged to them. The following passage from the *Atharva Veda* typifies their attitude.

Rightly I am the son of the Earth. The Earth is my mother. May the earth goddess who bears her treasure stored in many places, gold, gems, and riches, give opulence, grant great happiness to us, bestowing them with love.

When many things are offered to Agni or the god of fire in a yajna, to the accompaniment of chanted Vedic mantras, this is known as *homa*. Offerings to many gods are made through Agni, who is the mediator. Even though many divinities are mentioned, it would be wrong to label the Vedas as postulating polytheism. The Vedas emphatically proclaim that there is only one God and That has manifested as the different deities.

Performing any rite or ritual with a feeling of devotion as an offering to the Supreme can be termed a yajna, which is the meaning made clear in the *Bhagavad Gita*. Lord Krishna says that any activity of the human being that is intended to contribute something to the society with a selfless intention can be called a yajna. The entire eighteenth chapter of the *Yajur Veda* deals with this type of yajna, which is not a fire ritual. Rather, it refers to the human being's dynamic activity to explore and utilize Nature's resources for the benefit of all. Any coordinated, well-planned effort for the common good can be called a yajna. This is a sacred act and hence is known as a sacrifice or a selfless act.

The immortal soul assumes a human form for benevolent purposes. Man is not an individual. He is a social organism. God loves those who serve other beings, whether human beings, animals, or plants. An individual's glory lies in being a member of a big family. Though we have our personal blood relationships, we are in fact linked with every individual, whether near or far. The human being thus lives, works, and dies for society. We are expected to develop our craft, sciences, and technology and lead society from poverty to prosperity. Through a series of such lives, we are expected to attain our fullness, or liberation. In that state we shall revert to our self-effulgent form and enjoy divine bliss.

When a mantra for a certain deity is chanted, it calls forth that particular deva or deity. Spiritually evolved persons can see the deities or feel their presence when the mantras are chanted. These subtle divine forces that exist in Nature help humans to conduct their lives in the proper way and also fulfill their desires. The Vedas teach that they will be more inclined to help us if we worship them and offer libations to them. Thus, Lord Krishna says in the *Bhagavad Gita*:

Do thou worship the devas through yajnas and let them bring you prosperity by giving rains and such things. Thus helping each other, you will both prosper.

Every breath we take is part of the universal breath and every breath we give out is our contribution to universal life. This *prana,* this life force, is the same in everything and everyone and is spread everywhere simultaneously. Our lives can only become perfect if we participate in this great interchange with the universe. As the *Bhagavad Gita* tells us in the third chapter, *sahayajna praja srishtva purovacha prajapati*: "The Creator created all of us and instilled the idea of yajna or selfless action in us." No man is an island and no one can live without some sort of dependence on others and on Nature. *Ahamtva* and *mamatva* ("me" and "mine") have always been considered to be the two knots that alienate us from God. There is no "me" and "mine" as we think; rather, all things are connected in an amazing way to the unified field.

Similarly, quantum physicists have observed that subatomic particles have no meaning by themselves in isolation but only in relationship with everything else. Matter, at its elemental level, which is the quantum level, cannot be chopped up into intelligible units but is completely indivisible. If we want to understand the universe, we have to see it as a dynamic web of interconnectedness.

As Lynne McTaggart says in her book *The Field:*

Human beings are a coalescence of energy in a field of energy which is connected to every other thing in this universe. This energy field is the central engine of our being. We can never be estranged from the other aspects of this universe since we are all bound fundamentally to this field!

This was indeed the teaching of the Vedas, which they endeavored to establish in the life of the individual in a practical way through yajnas and rituals.

THE PERFECT LANGUAGE FOR SCIENCE

Another important point about the Vedas is the language in which they were written. Just as Hinduism is the oldest of all religions, Sanskrit is the oldest living language in the world. No one knows how it came into being or who made it. All languages have their origin in time and space and keep changing with the changing times and places in which they are spoken. But right from the first verse of the *Rig Veda,* the Sanskrit language has not changed: there has been no sound shift, no addition, no inspiration, and no change in import. The word Sanskrit means "perfect" and it was perfect from the time it came into being. It has not evolved from some initial imperfection. It exists now as it did before the dawn of history. It has mathematical precision and therefore zero deviation.

The question about its origin cannot be answered since its beginning is shrouded in mystery as with the Vedas. The scriptures say that Sanskrit came from the primary sound called *pranava* or *Aum* through which the Divine descended in order to create the world of the seen and the heard. The primary concern of other languages is communication through the *vaikhari* (spoken) medium. This is considered to be an inferior mode of communication in the Sanskrit-Vedic tradition. Sanskrit sounds are not merely meant for verbal communication but for removing the gross wrapping of materialism and exposing us to the vibrations of the divinity underlying all creation. It is most lyrical and poetic; it stirs the divine chords within us and helps us to align ourselves to the positive vibrations of Nature.

In other languages, words are not properly defined and are therefore ambiguous. Those languages are not natural since they are human based. Sanskrit, however, is precise, totally free of all ambiguity, and therefore most suited for computers, as was reported in *Forbes Magazine* (July 1987): "Sanskrit is the mother of all the European languages. It is the most suitable language for computer software."

Sanskrit is the most phonetic language in the world. The meaning of many Sanskrit words can be known through the sound they produce. Innumerable words are created with the help of seed sounds called *dhatus.* The Sanskrit language represents the thoughts, traditions, and cultural heritage of the whole of India. It is not the language of a community or a special region, but it has been the golden thread that has connected the whole of India into a single unit. As such the government has a duty to see that it is kept alive and taught in all schools. Scholars abroad have discovered that the learning of Sanskrit aids the growth of memory in children and there are many schools in the UK which teach Sanskrit to their students.

THE SIX SYSTEMS

Traditional Hindu philosophers continually emphasized the crucial importance of clearly understanding what Hinduism proper was. Two Sanskrit terms they repeatedly employed were *vaidika* and *avaidika.* The word *vaidika* (or "Vedic" in English) means "one who accepts the teachings of the Veda." It refers specifically to the unique stand taken by the traditional schools of Hindu philosophy, known as *sabda pramana,* meaning employing the divine sound current of the Veda as a means of acquiring valid knowledge. In this sense the word *vaidika* is employed to differentiate those schools of Indian philosophy that accept the epistemological validity of the Veda as a perfect authoritative spiritual source, eternal and untouched by the speculations of humanity, as against the avaidika schools that do not ascribe such validity to the Veda. In pre-Christian times Buddhism, Jainism, and the atheistic Charvaka schools were all known to be avaidika—not accepting the Veda. These three schools were unanimously considered non-Vedic, and thus non-Hindu. Though they are geographically Indian religions, they are not Hindu religions theologically and philosophically.

Historically speaking, there are six systems of Hindu philosophy that accept the Veda as their main source of valid knowledge about spiritual matters. These systems are known as *darshanas.* In Sanskrit, *darshana* means a "point of view" or "a method of looking." It is interesting to see how scientific many of these ancient systems were. The founders of these systems were great rishis in their own right, who had a deep insight into the workings of nature; hence they can be called scientists. They photographed truth from various angles as it were, accepting the fact that truth is many-faceted.

1. The Sage Gautama is the founder of the Nyaya philosophy, which deals with logic and reasoning. In fact, all Hindu logic is derived from his work.

2. Kannada is the founder of the Vaisheshika school, the first ancient school in the world to deal with atomism. He decreed that the world is composed of atoms long before the atomic theory was even thought of. He talks of *anus* (atoms) and *paramanus* (molecules). Vaisheshika makes use of Nyaya logic, and these two schools are closely connected.

3. The great sage Kapila is the founder of the Samkhya philosophy, which postulates Reality as being dual, Prakriti and Purusha or Nature and Spirit. He postulates that the world is made up of the five great basic elements. To these were added many others, making up a total of twenty-four cosmic principles. The basics of the Samkhya system were later used by both Yoga and Vedanta.

4. Patanjali, the founder of the Yoga school, was the greatest psychologist known to the world. He taught the various methods of mind control like meditation and breath control, which are still used by all those who wish to attain liberation. Samkhya and Yoga are always connected.

5. Mimamsa is differentiated into two schools, one of which is known as Purva Mimamsa, which was founded by the sage Jaimini. It stresses the efficacy of that portion of the Vedas that advocates yajnas and other rituals.

6. Uttara Mimamsa is another name for Vedanta, the path of wisdom taught in the Upanishads. There are three schools of

Vedanta, each having its own teacher or guru. Adi Shankara is the founder of Advaita Vedanta, which is the most famous of all the schools. He says that Reality is One alone and is called Brahman. This is known as monism. Ramanuja is the founder of the Visishtadvaita school of qualified monism. Madhvacharya is the founder of the school known as Dvaita or dualism.

Knowledge, scriptures, and discourses cannot disclose the cause of life. Do thou search for the wisdom of existence in the eternal reality that unites life.

MUNDAKA UPANISHAD

When the earliest of mornings dawned, the Great Eternal was manifested as the path of light. Now the commands of the devas shall be revered. Great is the One source of energy of the cosmic forces.

RIG VEDA 3.55.1

Beyond all senses, mind, intellect, and ego is the essence of existence, the ultimate cause. One who realizes that endless entity is relieved from the cycle of birth and death. The unborn Supreme Self is beyond all descriptions. Scriptures and speculation give us no clue. The right path alone can take us to the wisdom that reveals its undeniable presence in all mortal beings.

KATHA UPANISHAD

Loka Samasthath Sukhino Bhavantu!

Aprameyaaya Namaha!
Salutations to the Immeasurable!

3

Brahman and Atman
The Wave Is the Ocean

If there is one place on this earth where all the dreams of living men have found a home from the very earliest days when man began the dream of existence, it is India.

ROMAIN ROLLAND,
FRENCH PHILOSOPHER, 1886–1944

By getting to smaller and smaller units, we do not come to fundamental units, or indivisible units, but we come to a point where division has no meaning.

WERNER HEISENBERG

Before we go into the actual teaching of this chapter, it would be good to clear up any possible confusion arising from the word *Brahman*. There are quite a few words that sound and are spelled similarly, so let us try to differentiate between them.

Brahma is the Creator in the Hindu trinity consisting of Brahma, Vishnu, and Shiva.

Brahman is the Ultimate Advaitic (nondual) Reality of Hinduism. It is the immutable self-existence on which all that moves and evolves is founded. Its counterpart or reflection in the human being is known as the Self or *atman*.

Braahmanas constitute the second portion of every Veda and give details about how yajnas and other fire rituals are to be conducted.

A brahmin or a braahmana belongs to the highest, priestly class of the ancient Vedic caste system. They were so-called because they were the custodians of the Vedas and thus had to be highly enlightened souls who were actually knowers of Brahman.

EXPRESSING THE INEXPRESSIBLE: *SAT-CHIT-ANANDA*

The highest doctrine of the Sanatana Dharma as given in the Advaita Vedanta school of Hinduism declares that the Ultimate Reality is nondual (*advaita*) and is that which supports both the manifest and unmanifest states of creation. The *Katha Upanishad* says, "All the Vedas together talk of a single Being." What is that Being? The Vedas declare it to be that which is represented symbolically by the sound *Aum* ॐ.

This Reality is an integrated state which is changeless, indivisible, and beyond human comprehension, beyond space and time. We cannot use any language for Brahman since it is not an object. Though we use the word *Brahman,* the fact is that it does not help us to conceptualize It. Brahman is formless and therefore does not occupy space. Anything that maintains form and position expends energy. Anything that has qualities has some action and action cannot be accomplished without expenditure of energy. Anything that spends energy undergoes modification. Brahman, being immutable and eternal, has no form, no qualities, and no functions. Being changeless, It does not undergo decay, and being imperishable, It does not grow. It is One without a second. It is nonrelational so there is no question of anyone perceiving It.

The human mind cannot comprehend that which is totally without attributes so the rishis have described It as *sat-chit-ananda—* existence-consciousness-bliss.

Existence: Sat

Brahman is the supracosmic force that sustains the cosmos of living and nonliving beings. Brahman alone is, and because It exists, everything else exists, for everything is in its essential nature nothing but Brahman. Thus the first attribute of Brahman is that It is pure existence or *sat*. Everything else is a superimposition on It. Brahman is imperishable, changeless, steadfast, and eternal. It is the only Reality. Everything else is unreal inasmuch as everything else is transitory, ephemeral, and elusive.

Many centuries before Einstein, our rishis pointed out that the universe of forms is relative. Einstein said, "Everything is relative, nothing is absolute." The Advaita Vedanta of Hinduism says, "Only the Absolute is real, everything else is relative!" Even in this modern age many people cannot understand this. It is only the rishis and the scientists who can appreciate such a statement.

Consciousness: Chit

Brahman is also pure consciousness, *chit*—that consciousness that knows itself in all that exists. Chit or *chaitanya* is not a product of anything. It is the nature of the Supreme Reality and the primary substratum of everything. Consciousness is not an attribute of Brahman since It has no attributes. Vedanta says that Brahman is an undifferentiated, homogenous whole of consciousness—*prajnaaghanam* (filled with consciousness).

Before the manifestation of the world, there was no matter and no energy. The world did not come out of nothing. The positive entity that ever exists and existed before the cosmic manifestation is not insentient. There is a grand design in the cosmic anatomy and physiology. For the maintenance of the cosmic processes, intelligent coordination, control, and execution are unavoidable. Thus, Hinduism says that Brahman is that super consciousness by which everything is kept under control. Brahman is consciousness in conscious beings and consciousness in inconscient things.

What happens in the empirical world is witnessed by that Pure Consciousness. Brahman is the only witness (*sakshi*) of the world play. After the dissolution of the universe, the relative existence disappears and only Brahman remains as the solitary witness of the void.

Bliss: Ananda

The third classification of Brahman is that it is *ananda,* the secret bliss of existence, which is the ether of our being and without which we cannot breathe or live. Even someone who is suffering terribly clings to life because of this element of bliss. Ananda has no opposite since it is a self-contained state of deep contentment, uncontaminated by opposites.

It is because everything contains all these attributes of Brahman that the world appears to exist and has consciousness and holds bliss. Thus the purport of all the Vedas is to make us realize by our own experience what Brahman is and thus live in a state of bliss.

KNOWING THAT

Now the question may be asked, if Brahman is the only Reality, how can It be said to pervade everything? What does everything imply? Here we have to differentiate between three types of realities. Brahman is known as the absolute Reality, which cannot be contradicted under any circumstances. The universe has only a relative or empirical reality, as its existence is dependent on Brahman. It is never stable and always changing. Finally, there is illusory reality such as a mirage in the desert.

"Waves," "ripples," and "surf" are only names that we give to the water in the ocean. They really have no separate existence; they are pervaded by water. Similarly, the world exists because of and is pervaded by Brahman. Brahman has no cause and is not the cause of anything else. It is not the agent or the material or efficient cause of anything.

Brahman is *avyakta,* not perceptible by the five senses, and *achintya,* that which cannot be thought of in the mind. Vedanta gives a very precise psychological and physical account of the process of any type of perception by any of the five senses. The sense organ receives the external stimuli and transmits it to a specific center in the brain. The brain gets a certain feeling, which depends on the particular center that is stimulated; that is our sensation. What happens in the brain center is not known by us. The sense organ, the conducting nerves, and the brain matter itself are all insentient. Despite this we get knowledge through this method. Vedanta says that knowledge is possible only due to the reflection of consciousness on the insentient organs. Because of the presence of *chit* (consciousness), the eye is able to see, the ear is able to hear, the nose is able to smell, the tongue to taste, the skin to touch, and the mind to think. Without the light of pure consciousness our sense organs are like clods of earth. This being the case, the senses by themselves are not able to cognize Brahman.

Brahman is self-effulgent, self-luminous (*svayam jyoti*). It illumines the whole universe and is not illumined by anything else. The sun, moon, stars, and other effulgent things like lightning are all illumined by the light of Brahman. Thus the *Bhagavad Gita* says about the state of Brahman—"There nothing shines—no sun, no moon, and so on." The effulgence of Brahman is such that even a thousand suns will not appear to be shining in Its presence, just as thousands of electric bulbs cannot be said to be effulgent in broad daylight!

It is time and timelessness, space and all that is in space, causality as well as cause and effect, the thinker and the thought, the warrior and his courage and his cowardice. At the same time it is not bound by time, space, or causality. Any nonchanging entity, ever free from modifications, is bound to be eternal, beyond the three periods of time—past, present, and future.

The scriptures made many attempts to describe Brahman by using contradictions. For example, the *Yajur Veda* says:

It moves, It moves not.
It is far and It is near,
It is within all this,
And It is outside all this.

The *Kena Upanishad* says:

Brahman is known to him who thinks he does not know It. He who thinks It is known to him does not know It. It is not understood by those who say they understand It. It is understood by those who do not understand It!

They also used the method of negation, by saying, *neti, neti*—not this, not this. Thus, the scriptures all declare that Brahman cannot be known through logic but even so the scriptures all ask us to know Brahman. How to know something that is unknowable? Actually this is not as difficult as it appears. At the end of all acts and rituals, we repeat the words *Aum Tat Sat*. This is to emphasize the truth that the Supreme alone exists and It alone is the truth. *Tat* means "That" or the Supreme and *sat* means "truth." By referring to It as "That," it does not mean that It is far away. The Brahman you are referring to as "That" is actually closer than the closest.

THE GREAT MANTRAS

The *mahavakyas* or great truths of the Upanishads give us the method of knowing this proximity. They teach us that the Self or the atman in each of us is nothing but the Absolute or Brahman. Of these, four are considered to be especially important; one is found in each of the Vedas.

The mahavakya from the *Taittiriya Upanishad* of the *Rig Veda* says,
prajnanam brahma—"Brahman is pure, divine consciousness."

The next mahavakya comes from the *Brihadaranyaka Upanishad* of the
Shukla Yajur Veda and states, *aham brahmasmi*—"I am Brahman."

The third mahavakya comes from the *Chandogya Upanishad* of the
Sama Veda and is *tat tvam asi*—"That thou art."

The fourth mahavakya comes from the *Mandukya Upanishad* of
the *Atharva Veda* and says, *ayam atma cha brahma*—"atma and
Brahman are one."

In the phrase "That thou art," the word *tat* or "that" stands for
Brahman and *tvam* stands for "thou" or the personal self. This mantra
could be changed into "Thou, thou art"—"you are you." If you remove
the idea of the world and the body and concentrate on your identity
with Brahman, it brings the immediate realization that you are nothing but Brahman. Hence the next mahavakya—*aham brahmasmi*—
"I am Brahman." That is the same as realizing that your own Self is
Brahman. Hence, the final mahavakya—*ayam atma cha brahma cha*—
"I am the atma, which is also Brahman."

When the great cosmic awareness dawns, you say, *atmaivedam
sarvam*—"All this is indeed the atma (self)"; *brahmaivedam sarvam*—
"All this is indeed Brahman." After this realization, the difference
between subject and object disappears; there is nothing like you and
I, seer and object. The knower, the knowable, and knowledge all melt
into one pure consciousness alone. Nothing else remains—*sarvam
khalvidam brahma*—"Everything is Brahman." All differences and
dualities disappear into the great melting pot of Brahman. This state of
consciousness is of course very rare and is known as cosmic consciousness. Ordinary consciousness has to reassert itself or else the personality will no longer be able to live in the physical world.

Thus *atma sakshatkara* or "Realization of the Self" is the same
as *brahma sakshatkara,* "Realization of Brahman." When you see the
world as Brahman, you are actually projecting your own Self into the

world and seeing the world as your own Self! Just think of what this implies. As the great sage Yajnavalkya told his wife Maitreyi:

> The husband loves his wife for the sake of the Self, the wife loves the husband for the sake of the Self, and the mother loves her child for the sake of her own Self.

So the love of the Self is the supreme love and there is nothing higher than this. When we project our Self into the world and see the whole world as nothing but a projection of our own beloved Self, it follows that we will love the whole world as our own Self. This is why enlightened souls have no difficulty in loving the whole of creation and dying for the sake of another if called upon to do so.

HERE AND NOW LIBERATION

What about the world that appears so real and solid to the majority of human beings? Has it no reality? Advaita Vedanta postulates that the world is a world of shadows (modern science has used the same words). It has as much reality as the dancing patterns that portray the drama of life on the unchanging TV screen. Without the immutable, colorless, unshaken screen behind, the show could not be projected. The show consists only of changing patterns of light. (Again this is what physics postulates.)

The rishis of old knew that this is a shadow world—a world of *maya* (illusion). But they asked the million-dollar question: "If this is a shadow world then what is the Being that casts the shadow?" A shadow obviously cannot exist on its own. All our scriptures have given the answer that there is a Being that is the cause of these shadows. This exists because That exists. If That were not to be, then "this" would cease to be. In the *Bhagavad Gita* Krishna declares, "All things exist in Me but, mark my mystery, I do not exist in them." Fish exist in the water but the water does not exist in the fish or because of the fish.

Fish cannot exist without water but water can and does exist without fish! What Krishna means to say is that Brahman is not a sum total of all creation. That is why no amount of inquiry into the shadow world can give us the truth of absolute consciousness.

In another simile Krishna says, "Everything is strung on me as pearls on a string." The necklace has a shape and value only due to the string that holds the pearls together. If the string is broken, the necklace will no longer exist. The pearls will roll around in a random fashion like negative particles.

Since Brahman is that Reality that enfolds us from birth to death and beyond, it follows that It should be available in this life. The aim of the Vedas and Puranas is to help us to gain moksha (liberation) while living in this world itself. This is the greatness of Hinduism. All other faiths talk of liberation only after death. No one has come back to give us an account of the state after death. Therefore, the Sanatana Dharma insists that this state can and must be attained while in this very world. The *Bhagavad Gita* says, *ihaiva thairgita sarge*—"Liberation must be attained here and now." "What use is liberation for us after death," asks Lord Krishna. If we apply ourselves to the dictates of the Vedas and the Puranas, of which the *Bhagavad Gita* is a classic example, we will attain this state in this very life itself. Hinduism goes to the very root of bondage, which is existence itself, and helps the individual destroy the sense of separation from the Supreme to provide a permanent release instead of a temporary cure.

Nowadays *enlightenment* has become a hackneyed word. Many novices who have read a little about the Upanishads and about Brahman (which is actually something like the quantum state but much deeper and more meaningful) try to mix up the two; whenever they get defeated in any argument they fall back on what is called the "Vedantic shuffle." They get out of a difficult position by saying that "everything is maya, so why bother?" Neither the Vedas nor the Vedanta supports this type of statement.

The rishis realized that the world as it appeared to the common man was totally different from what appeared to the realized soul. For us the world is real because we take whatever the five senses tell us as absolute truth. The enlightened soul, however, lives in what is known as a state of cosmic consciousness in which the whole world is experienced as pure consciousness. Therefore, the rishis taught that these two were separate worlds and should not be confused with each other. The rules that apply to one need not necessarily apply to the other.

The teacher or guru of the Upanishads insisted that students should be wary of mixing up the rules of the inner world and the outer. A funny story is often told to prove the point. A teacher had been telling his students that everything was Brahman: whatever you could see or touch or hear or smell and even beyond the senses. The students set out for a walk and saw a mad elephant rushing toward them. The elephant man sitting on top was shouting to people to get off the road. All the students except one took to their heels. The poor bewildered one stood in the middle of the road and said, "The elephant is Brahman and I am also Brahman. He will not hurt me." Of course the elephant did not know he was Brahman, so he came and took the poor boy in his trunk and tossed him like a straw to the side of the road.

Luckily, the boy survived, and when he returned to his guru, he complained bitterly, "You told me that everything was Brahman, so why did the elephant harm me?"

The guru said, "I have told you not to mix up the laws of one world with the other. Even if you did so, why did you not respect the advice of the elephant man who was also Brahman and who told you to keep off the path of the maddened elephant?"

In the Sanatana Dharma, Brahman is reflected in our own hearts as the Self or atman. So eventually our own consciousness has to be followed. We may refer to our guru or spiritual preceptor for guidance, but these gurus are chosen by our own selves, so even here the reference is to our own inner guide that will prompt us to choose. Gurus have to be enlightened souls who instinctively know who their disciples should be. When the great Indologist Paul Brunton went to Sri Chandrashekharendra Sarasvati, the saint of Kanchipuram, the sage told him to go to Thiruvannamalai where he would find his guru. He went there and met the great sage Sri Ramana Maharishi, who later became his guru. The guru knows the disciple's mentality and state of evolution and will give him the sort of spiritual guidance that is right for him.

The guru may not give the same teachings to all his disciples. There are no hard and fast rules in spirituality that can be followed by everyone indiscriminately without reference to his or her own needs and development. Hence, the *guru parampara* (lineage) is not an authoritarian command. Even after having chosen our guru, we should not follow blindly everything he says. We should bring the light of our own reason to bear on all things, including scriptural injunctions. But once we have tested and found our guru to be the one for us, we should follow his advice with faith and trust, since the guru knows our own abilities and nature better than we do.

Even so it should be understood that the guru only points out the way. He is not expected to carry us on his back. The whole responsibility of following his words and of choosing or rejecting the advice falls on us. Of course this imposes a strain on the individual. It is easy to blindly follow someone else's instructions about how we should behave but more difficult when the whole responsibility is put on ourselves.

> *I bow to that Para Brahman, which is Pure*
> *Consciousness,*
> *Unsullied, indestructible, desireless, formless, beyond the*
> *three gunas,*
> *Not perceivable, One alone, ever in the turiya state of*
> *consciousness,*
> *This can only be gauged through the mantra Aum.*
>
> RIG VEDA

Who knows what the truth is,
Or who may here declare it?
What is the proper path
That leads to the place of divine forces?
Only their inferior abiding places are perceived,
Not those that are situated
In superior mysterious locations.

Rig Veda

Loka Samasthath Sukhino Bhavantu!

Shantidaaya Namaha!
Salutations to the Giver of Peace!

4

The Upanishads
Revelations of Timeless Truth

Still there are moments when one feels free from one's own identification with human limitations and inadequacies. At such moments, one imagines that one stands on some spot of a small planet, gazing with astonishment at the cold yet profoundly moving beauty of the eternal, the unfathomable. Life and death flow into one and there is neither evolution nor destiny, only Being.

ALBERT EINSTEIN

In India I found a race of mortals living on the earth, but not adhering to it. Inhabiting cities but not being fixed to them. Possessing everything but possessed by nothing.

APOLLONIUS TYANEUS,
GREEK TRAVELER OF THE FIRST CENTURY CE

*Whence arises all the order and beauty we see in the
World.*

ISAAC NEWTON

The main theme of the Upanishads is a philosophical inquiry into the
nature of truth and the methods of controlling the mind by which this
truth can be realized. Though truth is a matter of direct realization
by one's own individual efforts, the rishis have gifted us the Vedas, a
vast and priceless literature relating the experiences and exhortations of
those who have gained direct realization of this truth. Foreign scholars who have read the Upanishads as a purely intellectual exercise have
not even been able to touch the fringes of that transcendental truth as
explained in the Upanishads. However, most of them have been struck
by the profound wisdom embedded in them.

The word *upanishad* can be broken up into *upa-ni-shad,* which
means "to sit by the side." Literally, the disciple sat by the side of the
teacher during the discourse. It can also mean "that which takes you
to the side of Brahman." The teachings of the Upanishads were esoteric teachings given only to those who were fit to receive them. The
special characteristic of the Upanishads is that they contain mantras
that transmute their import through vibrations into actual experiences.
They are such an important part of the Vedas that they are sometimes
referred as *shruti siras* or the head of the Vedas.

"From the words of the poet men take what meanings please them,
but their last meaning always points to Thee," said the great poet
Tagore. Similar is the case with the Upanishads. They are filled with
exquisite poems but—whatever their apparent meaning—they always
point to the Absolute Reality that is both within and without.

Many Upanishads must have existed but only 108 are available to
us now. Among these, ten have been depicted as most important since
Adi Shankaracharya, the founder of the Vedantic school of philosophy,
wrote commentaries on them. These ten are *Ishavasya, Kena, Katha,*

Prasna, Mundaka, Mandukya, Taittiriya, Aitareya, Chandogya, and *Brihadaranyaka.*

The Upanishads are given in the form of guru-disciple discourses. The disciples would sit close to the guru and ask him questions. The latter would answer them and then ask questions of his own, which were very often abstruse. The questions were always meant to make the student delve within and discover the answers for himself. The answers were never given on a plate. The disciple had every right to question the teacher and argue with him if necessary until he was intellectually satisfied that what the guru had said was right. Very often the guru would give contradictory advice to different students depending on their level of understanding. The famous hymn that was always chanted at the beginning of a session shows how the teacher accepted the student as an equal.

Aum sahanavavatu.
Sahanabhunaktu.
Saha veeryam karavavahai.
Tejasvinaavadheetamastu, ma vidwishavahai.
Aum shanti, shanti, shanti.

May he protect us.
May he take pleasure in us.
May we perform great deeds together.
May spiritual knowledge shine before us.
May we never have occasion to disagree with
      each other.
May peace, peace, peace be everywhere.

ISHAVASYA UPANISHAD

The *Ishavasya Upanishad* comes at the end of the *Shukla Yajur Veda Samhita.* It begins with the famous couplet:

Ishavasyamidam sarvam yadkim cha jagatyam jagat.
Everything that you can think of in this universe is filled with
God alone. Claim nothing and enjoy. Do not covet His property.

Another oft quoted couplet from this Upanishad is:

Aum poornamada, poornamidam, poornath poornamutachyate,
poornasya, poornamaadaaya, poornamevavashishyathe.
That is full. This is also full. Fullness can come only from fullness.
Take away the full from the full and fullness will still remain.

Three other quotes are:

They have put a stopper in the neck of the bottle. Pull it out O
Lord and let out Reality. I am full of longing.

Unmoving, It moves; It is far away, yet near, within all, yet
outside all.

Of a certainty, the man who can see all creatures in himself,
himself in all creatures, knows no sorrow.

KENA UPANISHAD

The *Kena Upanishad* comes in the *Sama Veda*. *Kena* means "what" or
"at whose command?"

The student questions the teacher, "What has called my mind to
the hunt? What has made my life begin? What wags in my tongue?
What god has opened my eye and ear?"

The teacher answers:

It lives in all that lives, hearing through the ear, thinking through
the mind, speaking through the tongue, seeing through the eye.

That which makes the tongue speak, but which no tongue can explain, that which makes the mind think, but needs no mind to think, that which makes the eye see but which needs no eye to see, that which makes the ear to hear but which needs no ear to hear, that which makes life live but needs no life to live—that alone is the Spirit!

One who says he knows the atma, knows it not, one who says he knows it not, knows it. One who says he sees it, sees it not.

It is interesting that the *Kena Upanishad* is the only Upanishad in which the goddess makes an appearance. She is supposed to be especially fond of Sama Gaana, the music of *Sama Veda,* so it is befitting that she makes her emergence in the *Sama Veda.* The gods in their arrogance failed to find the Supreme Reality so the goddess appears in the form of Divine Wisdom and imparts the Supreme Wisdom to Indra, king of the gods. She discloses the fact that all our powers are derived from Para Shakti, the mysterious power of Brahman.

The goddess tells the gods:

All of you have attained your greatness through the Supreme Spirit. Do thou praise the glory of that Spirit.

Austerity, self-control, meditation are the foundation of this knowledge. The Vedas are its house, truth, its shrine.

KATHA UPANISHAD

The *Katha Upanishad* comes in the *Krishna Yajur Veda* and is in the form of a story. In fact *katha* means "story." It begins with the famous mantra mentioned above, which is chanted before starting any teaching.

The Upanishad expounds many great truths in the form of a dialogue between Yama, the God of Death, and the boy Nachiketas, son of a king. The idea of the *jivanmukta* or the soul that is liberated even while living in the body is also found here. The boy Nachiketas asks for three boons from Yama, the God of Death. Of these, the third one is the most interesting.

He asks, "Some say that when a man dies he continues to exist, others that he does not. Explain and that shall be my third gift."

Who else but the God of Death would be the most competent person to tell us about the nature of death? Yama tries his best to avoid this question, but the boy is adamant and thus Yama tells him:

The senses are made to turn outward and therefore man looks outward, not into himself. Now and again a daring soul, desiring immortality, has looked inward and found himself. The ignorant man, running after pleasure, sinks into the entanglements of death, but the wise man, seeking the undying, does not run after things that die. He, through whom we see, taste, smell, feel, hear, enjoy, and know everything, he is that Self.

That boundless Power, source of every power, manifesting itself as life, entering every heart, living there among the elements, that is the Self.

When that Person in the heart, no bigger than a thumb, is known as maker of past and future, what more is there to fear? That is the Self.

This Upanishad also says: "Death may put out some lamps but the light of life is kept burning eternally." The death of an organism does not destroy the essence of life in it. In fact, Hinduism postulates that even when *pralaya* or annihilation of the world occurs, which modern science calls nuclear fusion, the essence of life would return to the original galactic storehouse for another cycle of life and death. Similarly, the consciousness that leaves the body at the time of death continues to keep the light of life burning somewhere else. Our children do not perish when we die. They carry on the torch of consciousness to future generations.

The motto that Vivekananda quoted—"*Utthishtata! Jagrita!* Arise, awake! Learn at the feet of the Masters. It is a hard path, the sharp edge of the razor!"—was from this Upanishad.

Many of the examples given by Lord Krishna in the *Srimad Bhagavad Gita* are found in this Upanishad.

> The Self knows all. It is not born, does not die, is not the effect of any cause. It is eternal, self-existent, imperishable, ancient. How can the killing of the body kill it? He who thinks that he kills and he who thinks that he is killed is ignorant. He does not kill nor is he killed.

The analogy of the upturned peepul tree found in the *Bhagavad Gita* is also from this Upanishad.

> Eternal creation is a tree with roots above, branches on the ground, pure eternal Spirit, living in all things and beyond which none can go—that is the Self.

The imagery of the body as the chariot is also found here.

> The Self rides in the chariot of the body, the intellect is the firm-footed charioteer, the discursive mind, the reins, the senses are the horses, and the objects of desire, the path.

PRASNA UPANISHAD

The *Prasna Upanishad* is one of three that come in the *Atharva Veda*. *Prasna* means "inquiry." It recounts the story of six sages who went to the Sage Pippalada and asked six questions to which he gave answers.

"Who created everything?"

The sage answered, "God created the world and he who recognizes him as such gets whatever he wants from the world."

"What power made the body? What gave it life? Which is the greatest?"

"May life, Master of the three worlds, protect us as a mother protects her children. Grant us wisdom, grant us luck."

"When does life begin? How does it get into the body? How does it get out of the body?"

"Life falls from the Self as shadow falls from man, Life and Self are interwoven. Life comes into the body so that desires of the mind may be satisfied. He who knows the source and power of life, how it enters, where it lives, how it divides itself into five, how it is related to the Self, attains immortality."

"Who is the waker, sleeper, dreamer, and enjoyer in man's body? On whom do they depend?"

"As the rays of the setting sun gather themselves up into his orb to come out again at sunrise, the senses gather themselves into the mind and the man is said to be asleep. When they come out again, he is said to be awake. When the mind is lost in the light of the Self, it dreams no more. It is lost in happiness. My son, all things fly to the Self as birds fly to the tree for rest."

"Lord, where does the man go after death, if he meditates on *Aum* all his life?"

"*Aum* is the conditioned and unconditioned Spirit. The wise man with its help alone attains the one or the other.

"He who meditates on the three syllables A, U, M, as upon God, is joined to the light of the sun. Peeling his negativity off as the snake peels off its skin, he goes through that light to the Kingdom of Heaven, to the God who is greater than the greatest of all creatures though living in our body."

MUNDAKA UPANISHAD

The *Mundaka Upanishad* also comes in the *Atharva Veda*. *Mundaka* means "shaven head," and this Upanishad is followed mainly by *sannyasins* or renunciates who have shaven heads. The following famous *shloka* comes from this Upanishad:

> May our ears hear only good, may our eyes see only good, and may we serve him with the whole strength of our body. Throughout our life, may we carry out his will. May peace, peace, peace, prevail on earth.
>
> As the web springs from the spider and is again withdrawn, as the plant springs from the soil, hairs from the body of man, so springs the world from the Eternal.
>
> He looks at all things; knows all things. All things, their nourishment, their names, their forms are from his will. All that he has willed is right.
>
> The sparks, though of one nature with the fire, leap from it; uncounted beings leap from the Everlasting, but these my son, merge into it again.
>
> The Everlasting is shapeless, birthless, and breathless, without a mind, above everything, outside everything, inside everything.

Also found in this Upanishad is the famous allegory of the arrow of the mind being shot at the target of Brahman and becoming totally dissolved in it.

> Take the bow of our sacred knowledge, lay against it the arrow of devotion, pull the string of concentration, and strike the target. *Aum* is the bow, the personal self (jivatma), the arrow, impersonal Self (Paramatma), the target. Aim accurately, sink therein.
>
> In a beautiful golden scabbard hides the stainless, indivisible, luminous Spirit. Neither sun, moon, star, neither fire nor lightning, lights him. When he shines, everything begins to shine; everything in the world reflects his light.
>
> Spirit is everywhere: upon the right, upon the left, above, below, behind, in front. What is the world but the Spirit?

The beautiful allegory mentioned earlier of jivatma and Paramatma as the two birds sitting on one tree is in this Upanishad.

Two birds, bound to one another in friendship, have made their homes on the same tree. One sits still while the other pecks at the fruit.

The one who desires one thing after another, brooding over them, is born where his desires can be satisfied.

He who has found him seeks no more, the riddle is solved, desire gone, he is at peace. Having approached from everywhere that which is everywhere, whole, he passes into that Whole.

This verse is chanted when one goes to meet a saint: "As rivers lose name and shape in the sea, wise men lose name and shape in God, glittering beyond all distances."

The motto of our country, *satyameva jayate, naanrutam*—"Truth alone triumphs, not falsehood"—is also from this Upanishad.

MANDUKYA UPANISHAD

Next comes the *Mandukya Upanishad*, also part of the *Atharva Veda*. This is the smallest of all the Upanishads and contains only twelve mantras. But it is one of the most famous and most effective. *Mandukam* means "frog." Quite a few conjectures are given as to why it should have been called "The Frog Upanishad." Varuna was the rishi to whom this was revealed and it is said that he had taken on the form of a frog at one time.

Another and perhaps more plausible reason is that this Upanishad tells us how to leap like a frog from the first to the fourth step of consciousness without difficulty. The stages of consciousness are *jagrita,* the waking state, *svapna,* dream state, *sushupti,* deep sleep, and finally *turiya* or the fourth state, which is the underlying state of awareness of the Supreme. The Upanishad says that it is possible to reach this state in one leap like a frog by meditation on *Aum*.

Aum is also known as the *pranava mantra*. This Upanishad declares that one can experience the identity of the jivatma and Paramatma by meditating on the pranava mantra. That turiya state of nonduality is beautifully described here as *shivam/advaitam*—auspicious and nondual. This is the state into which all creation melts at the end of a certain period of time.

> The Self is the Lord of all, inhabitant of the hearts of all. He is the source of all; creator and dissolver of all beings. There is nothing that he does not know.
>
> The only proof of his existence is union with him. The world disappears in him. This is the fourth state of consciousness, the most worthy of all.
>
> This Self though beyond words is that supreme word *Aum*. Though indivisible, it can be divided into three letters, corresponding to the three conditions of the Self. The syllable "A" corresponds to the waking state, the second letter "U" corresponds to the dreaming state, and the letter "M" is the deep sleep. The fourth state of the Self corresponds to *Aum* as the one indivisible word. Thus *Aum* is nothing but the Self. He who understands this with the help of his jivatma merges himself into the Paramatma.

TAITTIRIYA UPANISHAD

All the mantras that are used in rituals are found in the *Taittiriya Upanishad*. It has three parts, the first of which is called Shikshavali. All aspects of imparting education are given in this portion. Precepts like *satyam vacha, dharmam chara*—"Speak the truth, follow dharma"—are found in this portion. Some other popularly quoted mantras from this Upanishad are:

Give with faith; if you lack faith, give nothing. Give in proportion to your means. Give with courtesy. Give to the deserving. Give as the lovers of God give.

Mother, father, teacher, and guest should be treated like divinities.

God lives in the hollow of the heart, filling it with immortality, light, intelligence. Where the skull divides and where it is customary to divide the hair, like the hollow where the gate of God swings like the uvula within the palate.

The Upanishad answers the question: If liberation from this mortal existence is the goal of life, why should one marry? The answer given is that it is our duty to pass on the torch of the noble teachings of the Veda to posterity.

The second portion of the *Taittiriya Upanishad,* known as Anandavalli, dissects the personality into different parts. The body is known as the *annamaya kosha* or the sheath of food, since the body thrives on physical nourishment. Inside this is the *pranamaya kosha* or the sheath of breath or life. Next comes the *manomaya kosha* or the mental sheath. The *vijnanamaya kosha* is the intellectual sheath, which gives us the power of reasoning. The *anandamaya kosha* is the sheath of bliss, which is at the core of all the rest. The Upanishad says that this is the natural state of the atman—the state of bliss or ananda. Like all the Upanishads, we are given advice on how to attain this state, which is actually our natural state.

He who denies the Spirit, denies himself, he who affirms it, affirms himself. This blissful Self is the soul of the knowing Self.

Everything is self-created. He is that essence. Drinking that essence, man rejoices. If man did not lose himself in that joy, he would not be able to breathe, He could not live. Self is the sole giver of joy.

He who knows that spiritual joy that mind cannot grasp, or tongue speak, fears nothing. Should he do wrong, or leave good undone, he knows no remorse. What he does, what he does not, is sanctified; what he does not, what he does, is sanctified.

The third portion of this Upanishad is called Brighuvalli, since it was taught by Varuna to his son Brighu. The father tells the boy to plunge into deep meditation and actually experience what he has been taught. Brighu does deep penance and comes up first with the idea that the annamaya kosha or the body is the ultimate truth. Continuing his penance, he progressively discards it and the other two sheaths, pranamaya and vijnanamaya, finally arriving at the state of bliss—anandamaya kosha, beyond which he cannot go. He thus concludes that this is the ultimate truth.

Bhrigu meditated and found that bliss is Spirit. From bliss all things are born, in bliss they live, toward bliss they move, into bliss they return. This is what Brighu, son of Varuna, found in the hollow of his heart.

He who knows this stands on a rock; commands everything; enjoys everything; brings up a family; gathers flocks and herds; grows famous through the light of the Spirit; is a noble man.

The Upanishad does not scorn a worldly life but insists that it is only by leading a dharmic (righteous) life that we can reach the final stage. It actually gives us advice on how important food is to us.

Respect food. Life is food; body lives on food; body is life, life is body; they are food to one another.

Bow down to Spirit as the sole object of desire, and thus become the goal of all desire; worship Spirit as the master of all and thus become the master of all!

AITAREYA UPANISHAD

The *Aitareya Upanishad* comes at the end of the *Aitareya Aranyaka*. The rishi Aitareya was the one who gave it to us. It tells us how the various elements take their places in the body.

> Fire is the characteristic of speech and entered the mouth, air in the character of scent entered the nose, sun in the character of sight entered the eyes, the four quarters in the character of hearing entered the ears; vegetation in the character of hair entered the skin, moon in the character of mind entered the heart, death in the character of *apana* (downward breath) entered the navel, water in the character of seed entered the loins.
>
> The Spirit thought, "How should I enter the body?" He opened the suture of the skull, entered through the gate that is called the gate of joy (*brahmarandram*). He found three places where he could live, three conditions where he could move— waking, dreaming, sleeping.
>
> He entered the body, named its various parts, and wondered if there could be anything there that was not Spirit and rejoiced to find there was nothing but himself.

This Upanishad gives us many interesting facts about how a *jiva* (embodied soul) takes birth in a particular woman's womb from the father and is born into the world and takes birth again and again in various wombs and worlds depending on its sins and merits (*papa* and *punya*). Liberation from this can only come with the realization of the Supreme.

First he becomes the seed of a man, which is gathered from all the limbs of the body. Man nourishes himself within himself as seed. When he ejects the seed into a woman, he himself is born. That is his first incarnation.

The seed merges in the woman's body. Because it becomes her body, it does not harm her. She nourishes the self of the man within herself.

Protect her, for she is protecting the seed. Before and after the birth of the child, man blesses the child, thus blessing himself. Man lives in his child. This is his second incarnation. The son being the father over again, carries the traditions of the family and the father, having completed his fate, exhausted his years, dies and is born again. This is his third incarnation.

It gives the interesting story of the sage called Vamadeva who came to know about all his various births while still in his mother's womb. As soon as he was born, he flew like a hawk into the void and refused to enter into another cycle of birth and death.

"When lying in the womb I understood how the gods worked. They put me into that iron-gated, hundred-gated, prison. But I fled quickly like a hawk."

Vamadeva thought to himself, "On whom should I meditate?"

He is Spirit, Creator, God, all gods, earth, air, water, wind, fire, constituents of life, all greater and lesser combinations; seminal, egg-born, womb-born, sweat-born, soil-born, horses, cows, men, elephants, birds, everything that breathes, movable, immovable, all founded upon, all moved by that one Intelligence. Intelligence is Spirit.

With this knowledge, Sage Vamadeva did all that he desired, left this world for the higher regions, became immortal . . . yea became immortal.

CHANDOGYA UPANISHAD

The two largest Upanishads—the *Chandogya* and the *Brihadaranyaka*—are together as big as the other eight. *Chandogya* means "one who sings the Sama hymns." Of course this Upanishad comes in the *Sama Veda*. Just as the allegories used in the *Katha Upanishad* are largely used in the *Bhagavad Gita,* so also the Chandogya mantras are used in the *Brahma Sutras* of Vyasa.

Chandogya Upanishad contains many interesting stories. The brahmin boy Svetaketu, son of Uddalaka Aruni, was swelling with pride at his birth and knowledge. His father humbled him by various tests.

"I shall teach you that by knowing which you will have known everything."

"How is that possible?" asked the son.

"By knowing one nugget of gold you will know all things made of gold. They differ only in name and form. Their reality is gold alone.

"Remember, my son! The body bereft of Self dies. The Self does not die.

"That Being is the seed, all else but his expression. He is Truth, he is the Self.

"O Svetaketu! Thou art that! *Tat tvam asi!*"

Uddalaka then asked his son to fetch a banyan fruit and break it and take one small seed. He then asked him to break that seed and see what was inside that.

"I see nothing, Lord!" said the boy.

Uddalaka said, "My son! This great banyan tree has sprung up from a seed so small that you cannot see it. That Being is the seed; all else are but his expressions. He is Truth, he is the Self. Thou art That, O Svetaketu! *Tat tvam asi!*"

Uddalaka said, "Put this salt into water and see me tomorrow morning."

Next morning he asked Svetaketu to bring the salt he had put into the water.

Svetaketu looked but could not find the salt. The father now asked him to taste the water from the top, the middle, and the bottom, and he found that everything was salty.

Uddalaka said, "My son, though you do not see that Being in the world, he is here. That Being is the seed, all else is but his expression. He is Truth, he is the Self. Thou art That, O Svetaketu! *Tat tvam asi!*"

Tat tvam asi is one of the mahavakyas mentioned earlier.

This Upanishad also contains many interesting stories. Satyakama was born into a low caste family but longed to receive instruction from a great guru. In those days only brahmins were given instruction in the Vedas, but since he did not hide the fact of his lowly birth, his guru accepted him. Only a true brahmin, he said, would tell the truth, even though this might disqualify him for discipleship.

The story of the sage Narada is also told here. Even though he knew all the *shastras* (scriptures), he had not understood the truth of the atma. The secret is taught to him by the sage Sanatkumara. The sage tells him to start from *ahara shuddhi* or purity of food, which would lead to purity of mind and intellect, which would eventually lead him to union with the Supreme.

Pure food creates pure intellect. Pure intellect creates strong memory. Strong memory cuts all the knots of the heart.

Sanatkumara's description of Brahman:

He is below, above, behind, in front, on the right, on the left; he is everything. If I put the word "I" instead of "he," I can say, "I am below, I am above, I am behind, I am in front, I am on the right, I am on the left, I am everything." If I put the word "Self" instead of "he," I can say, "The Self is below, above, behind, in front, to the right, to the left. The Self is everything. The personal Self is the same as the impersonal Self. *Atma* and Brahman are equal."

Sanatkumara continues:

He who knows this cares nothing for death, cares nothing for disease, cares nothing for misery, and looks at everything with the eye of the Self, gets everything, goes everywhere, yet remains one, though multiplied threefold, fivefold, sevenfold, elevenfold, hundredfold!

The description of the Self as the space in the heart is given here.

In this body, in this town of the Spirit, there is a little house shaped like a lotus and in that house there is a little space. One should know what is there.

What lies in that space does not decay when the body decays, nor does it fall when the body falls. That space is the home of the Spirit. The Self is there, beyond decay and death, sin and sorrow, hunger and thirst. His aim is truth. His will is truth. Man can live in the body as long as he obeys the law, as a man may live in a farm or a town or province, if he obeys the law.

This body is under sentence of death. Nevertheless it is the house of the immortal, the unembodied. As long as he is in the body, he likes and dislikes. As long as he is in the body there is no escape. When he has cast off the body, likes and dislikes do not touch him.

BRIHADARANYAKA UPANISHAD

Briha means "large" and *Brihadaranyaka Upanishad* is the largest of all
the Upanishads. Normally, all Upanishads with the exception of the
Ishavasya come at the end of the Aranyaka portion of their respective
Veda. That is one reason why they are called Vedanta, or the end of the
Vedas. However, the *Brihadaranyaka* replaces the whole Aranyaka por-
tion of the *Shukla Yajur Veda*.

It includes the famous mantra, *asato ma sad gamaya, tamaso ma
jyotir gamaya, mrityor ma amrutam gamaya*—"Lead me from the unreal
to the real, from darkness to light, and from death to immortality."

This Upanishad contains six chapters. The first two chapters are
known as "Madhu Kanda." *Madhu* means "honey" and it refers to the
sweet juicy stage of bliss. The one who has experienced the atman will
feel the whole world to be sweet like honey. The world also will find
that such people are sweet.

> The Self entered into everything, even the tips of the fingernails.
> He is hidden like the razor in its case. Though he lives in the
> world and maintains it, the ignorant cannot see him.
>
> When he is breathing, they name him breath; when speaking,
> they name him speech; when seeing, they name him eye, when
> hearing, they name him ear, when thinking, they name him
> mind. But he is not wholly there. All these names are the names
> of his actions.
>
> Even today, he who knows that he is the Spirit, becomes Spirit,
> becomes everything. Neither gods nor men can prevent him for
> he has become themselves.

This Upanishad uses the method known as *neti, neti,* "not this, not
this," in order to get to the truth of the atman. By negating all the
lower worlds and the different personality sheaths, one can eventually

get to the truth of the Supreme. This realization leads to the feeling that this phenomenal world and all the creatures in it are *anandarasa,* or the essence of bliss.

> They describe Spirit as "not this, not this." The first means there is nothing except Spirit, the second means "there is nothing beyond Spirit." They call the Spirit the Truth of all truths.

This Upanishad also gives two examples of women who were learned in debate. The woman named Gargi could discuss the nature of Brahman on an equal footing with the rishis in King Janaka's council.

The Sage Yajnavalkya had two wives, Kartyayani and Maitreyi. The former was an ordinary woman but the latter demanded from her husband that she be taught the truth of Brahman and thus he agreed to teach her. The teaching is put beautifully in the nature of a story as is found in many of the Upanishads. Yajnavalkya divides his wealth between his two wives and is ready to leave for life in the forest when he is stopped by Maitreyi. She begs him to tell her the nature of that happiness that is forcing him to leave the comfort of his house and family and take to the life of a recluse.

Maitreyi asks him, "Lord, if I were to get the wealth of the whole world, would it make me immortal?"

Yajnavalkya answers, "No! Your life will be like the life of the wealthy. There is no hope of immortality through wealth."

Maitreyi says, "What can I do with that which cannot make me immortal? Tell me what you know of immortality."

He then teaches her how to differentiate between love and attachment.

> The love that a woman bears to her husband and to her children, and the husband likewise to his wife and children, does not

rise from anything inherent in the object but from the feeling of satisfaction it gives to the person. This is because the very nature of the self or atman is love. Love toward any object is always mixed with hate or indifference or disgust. Some objects arouse a feeling of love and others of hate or disgust. However, when the Self or atman is realized, all things become equally dear.

It is certain that the wife does not love her husband for himself but loves him for herself only. The husband does not love his wife for herself but loves her for himself only. The father does not love his sons for themselves but loves them for himself only.

Maitreyi, a man does not love anything for itself, but loves it for himself only. This Self, O Maitreyi, deserves to be known. If the Self is known everything else is known.

The Self is dearer than all else, dearer than son, dearer than wealth, dearer than anything else. The Self is God. Therefore one should worship the Self as Love. Who worships the Self as Love, his love can never perish.

This earth is the honey of all beings; all beings are the honey of this earth. The bright eternal Self that lives in this body and the bright eternal Self that is in the earth are one and the same. That is immortality. That is Spirit. That is all.

O Maitreyi! He is the one who knows everything. So how can the knower be known?

Later on, Yajnavalkya went to the court of King Janaka and was questioned by various people including the female ascetic Gargi as well as the king himself. When questioned about the state of the person at the end of his life, he gives many interesting examples.

As a caterpillar, having reached the end of a blade of grass, takes hold of another blade, then draws its body from the first, so the Self having reached the end of his body, takes hold of another body, then draws itself from the first.

How should the person get freed from this circle of birth and death?

> When all the desires of the heart are gone, mortal becomes immortal; man becomes Spirit, even in this life. As the skin of a snake is peeled off and lies dead on an anthill, so this body falls and lies on the ground but the Self is bodiless, immortal, full of light, he is of the Spirit so becomes the Spirit. If a man knows that he is the Self, why should he hunger for a body?

One of the stories related in the last portion of this Upanishad shows us how the same advice can be interpreted by people according to their relative state of consciousness. Once the gods, humans, and demons approached the Creator, Brahma, and asked for advice. He merely gave the syllable *da* to all of them and left them to make what they would out of this cryptic advice. The gods, who were noted for their lack of self-control, took it as advice to practice *dama* or self-restraint. The humans, whose nature is always to accumulate property, decided that the grandsire's advice to them was to give *dana* or charity, and the demons, whose nature is noted for its cruelty, thought that Brahma had exhorted them to show *daya* or compassion.

Another rather strange mantra in this Upanishad tells us to take any pain as part of the penance extracted from us by Nature. In ancient times people used to perform many types of tapas or penance in order to get rid of their negative karmas (bonds accruing from action), but in modern times, none of us is capable of performing these great sacrifices. So Nature in her kindness gives us bodily illness and discomfort to reduce our karmic bonds. Thus, injury and disease should be regarded as a type of tapas, which is not self-imposed but given by a compassionate Nature. When we begin to embrace this perspective, we will develop the capacity to bear illness with fortitude.

The last chapter of the Upanishad gives the knowledge of the

Panchagni Vidya* and the duties of householders who desire to beget noble children.

SCIENCE APPROACHES
THE UPANISHADIC REVELATION

The scientific development of the modern age has not posed any threat to the metaphysical doctrines of the Upanishads. On the contrary, modern science is approaching nearer and nearer to Advaitic thought, thus allowing the modern mind to grasp its gist more easily. Previously, it could only be understood through a study of the Vedas.

In the beginning science was of the opinion that all substances on earth were different from each other. Then these substances were boiled down to seventy-two elements. The combinations of these were said to be the cause of the material world. Then came the atomic age in which the scientists discovered that the origin of all these seventy-two elements is the same—pure energy—which is known as Shakti in Hinduism. As the Divine Mother told the saints in the *Kena Upanishad,* Shakti is Pure Consciousness, which includes all knowledge and is the basis of all animate and inanimate creation.

The universal energy that atomic science has discovered is a universal consciousness, about which the Upanishads were talking thousands of years ago. It is known as that which is nondual (*advaita*). It is beyond the reach of the physicist as well as the philosopher. It manifests in this plurality of objects, which is our normal day-to-day experience. This is what is known as *dvaita* or duality. If duality was the absolute truth, there would be no need for us to consult the Vedas or the Upanishads. We need their help only because they point to and establish the

---

*The word *panchagni* means "five fires." This is a ritual that is practiced during Uttarayana, or the course of the sun toward the north—from January 14 to July 14. The person who wants to practice it has to sit in the middle of four fires, which are lit in all four directions. The blazing sun above is the fifth fire. This form of tapas is done for many days or months, as necessary, in order to subdue the five fires or passions of the mind. These are *kama* (lust), *krodha* (anger), *lobha* (greed), *moha* (desire), and *mada/matsara* (jealousy). These can also be overcome by practicing other forms of *tapas* (austerity), *dhyana* (meditation), and *dana* (charity).

fact that the individual soul (jivatma) merges with the Cosmic Soul (Paramatma) and becomes the Advaitic (nondual) Brahman. In this way the Upanishads are still far ahead of modern scientific research, which is still trying to find a universal basis for everything.

"Look at God's poem, it neither decays nor dies," says the Veda. Our thoughts only touch the fringes of this divine poem, which connects the entire universe and runs through all human beings like a thread that binds a necklace of beads. Now and again one bead might come in contact with that thread and recognize its divinity and the fact that it is joined to all the beads in the universe.

When one is united with the beloved, all physical and
mental boundaries disappear. Likewise, in self-realization,
we forget our separateness and merge with the Supreme Self.

BRIHADARANYAKA UPANISHAD

Anyone who is not shocked by the quantum theory has not
understood it.

NEILS BOHR

It seems hard to look into God's cards. But I cannot for a
moment believe that he plays dice, and makes use of telepathic
means, as the current quantum theory alleges he does!

ALBERT EINSTEIN

The divine melody, with uniform light,
Spreads over the whole world,
It disseminates the wisdom that inspires the brave,
And with this melody the pious devotees expand
Their field of knowledge.

RIG VEDA

Loka Samasthath Sukhino Bhavantu!

Paramatmaaya Namaha!
Salutations to the Supreme Self!

5

The Puranas and Itihasas
Legendary Sources of History, Psychology, and Science

The one Supreme Reality has been styled
By various names by the learned seers.
They call One by many names:
They speak of Him as Indra, the Lord resplendent,
Mitra, the surveyor, Varuna, the virtuous,
Agni, the adorable,
Garutatman, the celestial and well-sung,
Yama, the ordainer, Matarishvan, the cosmic breath.

RIG VEDA

India conquered and dominated China culturally for
twenty centuries without ever having to send a single
soldier across her border.

HU SHIH, FORMER AMBASSADOR OF CHINA
TO THE UNITED STATES

The Vedic age of Hinduism was followed by the Puranic age. The Vedas and Upanishads were not freely available to the common people. Even when they were available, they were incomprehensible to most since the language was obscure. So the great Puranic sages, like Vyasa and Valmiki, compassionately presented the truth of the Vedas in a more palatable and understandable language. In this way they sought to preserve the truths of the Vedas and popularize them. The Puranas magnify and simplify the pithy statements of the Vedas and Upanishads, elaborating upon them in the form of stories and anecdotes. The Upanishads open us to the path of knowledge (*jnana marga*) and the Puranas lead us to the path of devotion (*bhakti marga*). Both these paths lead to the same goal—the liberation of the mind from its social and biological conditioning and its expansion to unlimited freedom.

The *Vayu Purana* declares that we cannot appreciate the Vedas if we have not read the Puranas. The Vedic injunctions like restraint, patience, compassion, chastity, and other dharmas (virtues) were illustrated in the Puranas through the lives of the great and noble men and women. As a result of listening to these stories, people developed a desire to shape their own lives according to the dharmas that they portrayed. The religion followed by countless Hindus today is based on what is presented by Valmiki and Vyasa. Even though most have no idea of the great glories contained in the Vedas, they still strictly adhere to certain rites and rituals by following which they can progress on the scale of evolution.

The Puranas also present the idea that we are all in reality the Supreme Spirit. It is common to oppose a truth but impossible to resist a story. The stories created by the Puranic rishis were a device to circumvent the opposition of their listeners to the simple yet shocking truth of who they really were. Vyasa dramatized the revelations of the Upanishads and wove stories around them, which could become familiar and understandable even to the poorest intellect. In fact, even children could appreciate them. Vyasa declared that if you listen carefully to a story, you will never be the same again. A story can weave its way into your heart and break down the barriers you have erected between yourself and the Divine.

THE NEED FOR DEVAS AND AVATARAS

The concept of the one Absolute cannot easily be grasped by the mind of the human being because of the dichotomy created in the mind between the self and the world, and the world and God. But in the Puranas, the one God becomes many, and the truths of the Vedas are interwoven with the stories of the gods. The forms of the gods are actually filled with great spiritual and scientific wisdom. The Vedas speak of the supernal ether or *akasa* as the abode of *vac* or sound. This is the storehouse of all sounds and is the permanent place of the light of all lights. It is the cause of all causes. From this mass of formless light emerge the rays that fashion all forms during the course of evolution. *Deva* means "the shining one" and the gods or devas are emanations from this light. That formless light emits rays that weave into the forms and features of the various gods. India's spiritual vision has evolved through these forms.

Western-educated people are unable to understand the great truths underlying these forms and consider them to be the result of a puerile imagination. They condemn them to the sea of meaningless figments of superstition coming from primitive minds. Who could believe in gods with several heads and hands and even animal heads? This Western misconception can be compared to the ignorance that uneducated people have about the significance of mathematical symbols, taking them to be mere scribblings of an immature pen.

According to Puranic perception, a deity is a facet of Brahman, the Supreme Reality, which has a potential for infinite expressions. The human being is one of these expressions and is placed in an evolutionary stage that can take a leap forward and embrace this supreme unconditioned reality of Brahman. The forms of the gods are the aids by which the human mind can escape from the conditioned patterns of its own thoughts and evolve to higher levels. The divine forms of the gods are a kind of symbolic language like algebraic symbols, devised by the rishis to help and guide us in our evolutionary journey. The divinity enshrined in the form of the deity expands the consciousness of the earnest seeker to its maximum—to the unconditioned level of the Supreme that transcends all forms!

Scientists and even Western-oriented philosophers are only just beginning to understand and appreciate the deep psychological and metaphysical wisdom preserved and transmitted in the form of Puranic lore and legend. In these Puranas are found the life and teachings of the great *avataras* or incarnations of God. They indeed are the word (*Aum*) become flesh whenever virtue declines, as Lord Krishna declared in the *Bhagavad Gita: yada yada hi dharmasya glanirbhavati, dharma samsthapanarthaya sambhavami yuge yuge*—"Whenever this dharma declines O Arjuna, I incarnate myself, in order to reestablish this ancient dharma." The avatars are the life force flowing through humanity's collective body, the true homes of our consciousness, capable of taking us to that impersonal Absolute that our untutored minds cannot comprehend.

RECORDS OF ANCIENT HISTORY

The Itihasas or epics known as the *Ramayana* and the *Mahabharata* are also integral parts of the Hindu religion. They respectively tell the stories of Rama and Krishna, the most beloved of the Hindu gods, who are worshipped to this day. The actual meaning of *itihasa* is "thus must we live." An Itihasa explains the four Hindu goals of life: *dharma,* virtue or righteousness; *artha,* the acquisition of wealth; *kama,* pleasure; and *moksha,* liberation from this mortal life. Artha and kama, the two materialistic goals, are informed by the higher goals of dharma and moksha. Thus, if we follow dharma in our pursuit of both wealth and pleasure, it will lead us to moksha automatically. The need to follow dharma or the cosmic law is stressed in the epics as well as the Puranas.

The *Ramayana* was written by Valmiki, who is known as the first of all poets. The story of Sri Rama, who was an avatara or incarnation of Vishnu, is a book that has influenced the life of every Indian from north to south and has even spread throughout Southeast Asia. When Vyasa composed the *Mahabharata* epic, consisting of a hundred thousand couplets, Lord Ganesha is supposed to have written down the words as Vyasa dictated them. In it is found a part of the life of the great avatara Lord Krishna. The great advice of Lord Krishna to Arjuna, known as the *Srimad Bhagavad Gita,* containing the essence of the Upanishads, is found in the middle of this enormous book. The *Mahabharata* has been called the fifth Veda, as it contains the essence of all the scriptures. It is an authority on Indian culture and religion.

It is generally believed that India has no recorded history. But the *Ramayana* and the *Mahabharata* give a faithful account of the history of the India of the times when Rama and Krishna lived. Valmiki was a contemporary of Sri Rama, so the *Ramayana* is actually a firsthand account of the history of that age. Vyasa, Lord Krishna's contemporary, also gives a firsthand description of the historical events that took place during his time. Western history contains nothing to match the stories of the Itihasas and Puranas, which not only appeal to everyone but also help us to mold our characters. This is the heritage of every Indian, regardless of creed or religion, since both Rama and Krishna belonged to a period when the world had never heard of Mohammed or Christ.

When the Western missionaries first came to India, they were appalled by the possibility that—if the history given in the Itihasas was true—a glorious civilization existed in India at a time when Europeans were barbarians running around brandishing crude weapons. They realized that the only way they could force their religion on the country would be to cast scorn on the two great gods of Hinduism—Rama and Krishna. So they took pains to prove that they were purely mythical characters materialized by the fertile brains of Valmiki and Vyasa. Unfortunately, the Hindu elite believed them, since they were also inculcated with the false belief that all civilizations started with the Greeks.

However, Indian history as recorded by Valmiki in the *Ramayana* clearly states all the details of Rama's lineage. He belonged to the Surya Vamsa and was the sixty-fourth ruler of the Ikshwaku dynasty. The names of his predecessors are also given. What more proof is needed to establish his reality? Yet the Western historians were bent on proving him to be a myth. There are twenty-three places in India that have memorials to commemorate the events in his life. Thanks to modern techniques, today we can scientifically gauge the data found in the *Ramayana,* which proves that there did indeed exist a divine personality called Rama, who ruled India thousands of years ago.

Thanks to Valmiki's extraordinary astronomical observations, it is possible today to pinpoint the exact dates given in the *Ramayana.* Valmiki was not only the first poet; he was also the first Indian astronomer and thus the world's first astronomer. His study of planetary configurations has stood the test of time. The latest computer software has corroborated his calculations. Valmiki gives the zodiac sign of Dasaratha, Rama's father, as Pisces and his star as Revathi. Rama left for his exile at one of the conjuctions of these stars. Modern calculations have shown that this configuration took place on January 5, 5089 BCE. Valmiki says that Rama was twenty-five years old at that time. He also mentions the solar eclipse that took place at the time of Rama's fight with the *asuras,* Khara and Dhushana. He said that it was *amavasya* (new moon) and Mars was in the middle flanked by Venus on one side and Mercury on the other. When this data was fed into the software, it came out with the date October 7, 5077 BCE.

By following other planetary configurations as mentioned by Valmiki in other places, we can see that the demon king Ravana was killed on December 4, 5076 BCE. Rama completed his exile on January 2, 5075 BCE, in the bright phase (*shukla paksha*) of the month of Chaitra, the month of his birth, and returned to Ayodhya at the age of thirty-nine.

Now let us take a look at the life of Krishna. Luckily, recent investigations have unearthed many astonishing facts. They prove, for those who need proof, that our scriptures were absolutely correct in their description of the fabulous city of Dwaraka, built by Krishna as the stronghold of the Yadavas. They also prove that Krishna was indeed the superman or supreme incarnation of God as our scriptures declare.

The modern city of Dwaraka is in the Saurashtra region and is a great pilgrim destination since our scriptures declare it to be the seat of the Yadava clan and Lord Krishna's capital. However, according to the stories mentioned in many of the Puranas, like the *Mahabharata, Harivamsa, Vishnu Purana,* and so on, the fabled city of Dwaraka was washed away into the sea soon after the Lord left his mortal body, as he himself had predicted.

In 1983, some excavations were done outside the modern city of Dwaraka, which revealed the existence of a glorious city of ancient times. The most interesting discovery was that of a set of seven temples, built one on top of the other at different periods of time. The one at the bottom was the most interesting since it showed many pottery shards and seals that clearly pointed to the existence of a fantastic city at about the time mentioned in the *Mahabharata*. These findings encouraged the marine archaeology center of the National Institute of Oceanography to take up serious excavation work along the coast of the island known as Bet Dwaraka.

The strongest archaeological support for the existence of the legendary city of Dwaraka comes from the structures discovered in the late 1980s under the seabed off the coast of modern Dwaraka in the state of Gujarat by a team of archaeologists and divers led by Dr. S. R. Rao, one of India's most respected archaeologists. Conducting twelve expeditions from 1983–90, Rao identified two underwater settlements, one near the present-day Dwaraka and the other off the nearby island of Bet Dwaraka. This tallies with the two Dwarakas mentioned in the epic.

Another important find by the divers was a conch seal that established the submerged township's connection with the Dwaraka of the *Mahabharata*. The seal corroborates the reference made in the ancient text, the *Harivamsa,* that every citizen of Dwaraka had to carry such a seal for purposes of identification. Krishna had declared that only one who carried such a seal could enter the city. A similar seal has been found onshore.

Around the same time, archaeologists from other countries were also busy. From 1998–2001, many underwater explorations along the coast of the Bay of Cambay and off the coast of modern Dwaraka found evidence of a settlement deep under the sea. In seventy feet of water, archaeologists discovered sandstone walls and cobbled streets. Many clues also indicate that it must have been a bustling port. Ancient anchor stones give ample evidence of this. It must have been washed away by a tsunami or something similar. In fact, the *Mahabharata* gives an eyewitness account of the disappearance of Dwaraka under the horrified eyes of Arjuna.

Wood and pottery shards were found that can be dated back 32,000 years, again proving that the time spans given in ancient Hindu scriptures are true, even though most Westerners dismissed them as being absurd. The city had existed from 32,000–9000 BCE. This discovery proves that the life of Krishna is not mere mythology but it is a true, historical record of a towering personality who had lived on this holy land of India. For many years now, Western Indologists have deliberately shut their eyes to the glory that was ancient India, but hopefully these findings should help them to believe, if they want to believe!

Dr. Narhari Achar, professor of physics at the University of Memphis, Tennessee, has dated the Mahabharata war using astronomy and regular planetarium software. According to his research conducted in 2004–5, the titanic clash between the Pandavas and the Kauravas took place in 3067 BCE. Using the same software, Achar places the year of Krishna's birth at 3112 BCE. Actually, our Puranas set it at a far earlier date.

VISIBLE SIGNS OF THE INVISIBLE

The universe of innumerable forms is an expression of God's unconditioned freedom to take on any form he chooses. To limit him to only one form is a failing of the human mind. Worship of divine forms is part of the practical aspect of Hindu spirituality. Our mind has to learn to focus on some form that inspires us before proceeding to the formless. This is the experience of every sincere seeker. It is based on a great psychological truth. Conditioned as we are to so many forms in the world, the mind of the human being is incapable of concentrating on that which is formless. Thus, even worship and ritual in Hinduism are scientifically based.

The Puranas are studded with stories of an amazing variety of gods and goddesses who are dynamic expressions of the truth as presented in the Vedas. These stories are not mere fairy-tales but the revelations of the Puranic rishis. Vyasa saw the totality of Nature—both her outer, physical phenomena as well as her inner, invisible psyche. The word paintings of Vyasa have given us graphic details of the forms of the various gods, which have provided us with a fund of spiritual wealth from which countless Hindus have derived unfailing inspiration. These forms were evolved in Vyasa's mind while in a superconscious state in an attempt to give the common human being a glimpse into the truth ever blazing in his heart.

The symbols of the various gods like Ganesha and Hanuman are the visible signs for expressing the invisible. One who meditates on these symbols will be able to penetrate the subtle psychic presence in them and come to a comprehensive view of the totality from which they are derived. This is the truth underlying all the idols and even the bizarre forms of the gods with many arms and heads and so on. They translate the Infinite in terms of the finite and the spiritual in terms of the material. By fostering our faith in the symbols and form of the deities, we can establish a rapport between the deity and us that will help to draw us closer to the Supreme at which they point. For example, there is a beautiful posture of Shiva as the divine archer in which he kneels on the ground holding his bow and pointing his arrow to the heavens as if exhorting us to look above. In fact, all the gods are at one time or other meditating on the Supreme, thus showing us the important fact that they are only emanations from Brahman and derive their power from That alone.

Professor Eliade declares:

> Images, symbols, and myths are not irresponsible creatures of the psyche. They resound to a need and fulfill the function of bringing to light the most hidden modalities of our being.

Thus, many Puranas were written, allowing the truth to be photographed from different angles and from various standpoints so that it could be appreciated from diverse intellectual levels. In this unique way, Vyasa succeeded in reflecting the incomprehensible Supreme in the liquid poetry of his Puranic literature and created myriad forms for worship, suitable for a variety of different personalities.

Unfortunately, the numerous forms of the gods found in Hinduism have always been a stumbling block to those who have had a genuine interest in learning about the religion. Vedanta establishes the Supreme Truth as the formless Brahman. Then what is the necessity for so many gods? The formless has taken on forms only to cater to the weakness of the human mind, which is incapable of meditating or even thinking of that which is nameless and formless. The mind is bound by what is known as *nama* (name) and *rupa* (form). It is powerless to think of that which is beyond name and form. However, the human being longs to have contact with its Maker; thus Hinduism says that the formless "One" of the Vedas is capable of taking on innumerable forms. In fact, it would be a sacrilege to confine that Infinite to just one form, limited to one space and time. It is beyond time and space and can and will take on as many forms as the human being wants.

All of us are created in different models with different likes and dislikes. Hinduism gives infinite freedom to the individual to choose the type of form that he or she likes to worship. The Divine is capable of many roles and all roles at the same time. He can be many things and all things simultaneously and separately to all humankind. Such is the glory of this Being, the nature of which is beyond the grasp of the mind. The fact that human beings are created in different models with different personalities was well known to the Puranic rishis. It is totally unscientific to expect all of us to follow one single path and gain liberation. Our sages knew how important it was to create ideals of perfection for a society to help it to evolve. Vyasa was a great psychologist. The insistent message underlying all of Vyasa's forms was that all these forms would lead to the same formless Absolute! Thus, we see how very scientific Hinduism is and how consistent in its insistence on finding the supreme goal. Lord Krishna says in the *Bhagavad Gita,* "Whatever form my devotee worships with faith, I enter into that form and make his faith firm!" What a catholic statement this is— filled with compassion and wisdom.

CREATION, MAINTENANCE, AND DESTRUCTION

We often think that Advaita Vedanta only advocates meditation on the formless using the great mahavakyas from the Upanishads. But this is not quite correct. Adi Shankara, who was the greatest protagonist of Advaita Vedanta, established temples to many of the great gods of Hinduism in different parts of India. He has also written many hymns eulogizing these gods, all filled with devotion and love. The fact is that Advaita Vedanta does indeed recognize the existence of a creator, preserver, ruler, and controller of this phenomenal universe. How could it not? It is so obvious that this grand phenomenon of the cosmos must have some cause. The perfect order, attention to minute details, breathtaking beauty, unique design, and intricate workmanship presuppose a cosmic intelligence, which we cannot even imagine. Advaita calls this intelligence Isvara or God. This universe emanated out of That, is maintained for a certain period of time, and then reabsorbed into That. Hinduism has a genius for clothing the Infinite in infinite forms. These three duties of creation, maintenance, and destruction are given to the three main gods of Hinduism. The Creator in the Hindu trinity is known as Brahma (not to be mistaken for Brahman or the Absolute). Vishnu or Narayana is the principle of harmony, and Shiva is the lord of Destruction. Numerous incidents and stories are woven to interest the devotees of these gods and make them understand scientific facts in an easy way.

Brahma the Creator

In the transcendental world, it is Brahma who captures the vibrations of the Supreme at the beginning of every creation and manifests all creation. Science has proved that when certain sound vibrations are made near plants, they induce faster growth and higher yield. Some other vibrations retard growth. This shows that sound vibrations are capable of creation, preservation, and destruction. Thus, Brahma was able to create the whole universe with the Vedic sounds by his tapas or austerity. Since Brahma is a manifestation from Brahman solely for the purpose of creation, he has total mastery of the Vedas.

In Hinduism, creation is not linear as we find in the West. *Shrishti, sthiti,* and *samhara*—creation, maintenance, and destruction—follow each other in order in a cyclical manner. Each creation has its own Brahma and when he takes on a form, all the Vedic sounds are born in his heart. These show him the path of creation. Out of the infinite numbers of mantras in the Veda, only a few were revealed to the rishis. The *Yoga Shastra* says that the microcosm is only a mirror of the macrocosm and if the space that exists in the cosmos and the space that exists in our mind are unified, we will be able to hear the sounds in space. Only those who feel united with everything in the universe will be able to hear this.

Vishnu the Sustainer

Vishnu or Narayana is the Sustainer or Preserver in the Hindu trinity. His image is found in temples all over India. Vishnu embodies the source of beauty and order in creation. His body is the dark blue of limitless space and the galaxies hang from his neck like innumerable strands of jewels. His four arms show that he holds sway over the four quarters of the universe. His qualities draw forth love, forgiveness, beauty, and compassion for all creatures.

Usually he is represented as a handsome man of divine radiance who holds in four hands the symbols of power and beauty. One hand holds the conch, which emits the divine call to all people to awake to the divinity within. The *chakra* or wheel is the wheel of time, which is the only annihilator of all creatures. Another hand holds the *gada* or mace to punish wrongdoers and make them return to the right path. The fourth hand holds a beautiful lotus, the symbol of purity. The lotus has its origin in the dirt and muck of a pond but frees itself from all this and lifts up its face to the light of the sun. So also the human being, even though filled with animal passions, is capable of shaking these off and rising to the divinity within.

His vehicle is the cosmic eagle, Garuda. He rests upon the serpent of infinity called Ananta, floating on the cosmic waters, which is the field of all possibilities, in perfect peace, dreaming the dream of the world. He is universally kind, approachable, understanding, and serene. He is the protector who rescues us in time of need and supports and strengthens us from within when external resources fail. Vishnu has taken on many avataras or incarnations, since he is the one who has to save the world when any danger threatens. Though Vishnu is perfect and untouched by any pollution, due to his love for his creation he allows himself to be born as a human being and undergoes all the problems that a human being would have to face in order to help his devotees. Ten avataras are commonly mentioned but the *Bhagavad Purana* says that he has taken an infinite number of avataras. Every time one of his devotees needs him and calls out to him, he takes on an incarnation since the love he bears for this creation is unfathomable.

The ten avataras have a scientific basis. They are supposed to tell the story of evolution from aquatic creatures to amphibian to human and so on. Hence, the first avatara is that of the fish (*matsya*), then comes the tortoise (*kurma*), then the boar (*varaha*), then the man-lion (*narasimha*), then the dwarf man (*vamana*), the axe man (*parashurama*), the perfect man (Sri Rama), the strong man (Balarama), the totally evolved man (Sri Krishna), and finally the epitome of destruction (Kalki), who is yet to come or perhaps has already come.

From this we see that Vyasa had a very good idea of the theory of evolution, which is such a modern concept. The *Bhagavad Purana* gives the stories of all the great avataras of Vishnu and also the less well-known ones. It is the greatest of the Puranas and inculcates devotion in the hearts of its listeners.

Hinduism lays great stress on the repetition of the names of God, which is known as *japa*. The name of God is itself God since sound and form have a definite connection, according to the science of phonetics. The epic *Mahabharata* gives us the many names of Vishnu, which is a very famous hymn chanted daily in thousands of Hindu homes. The vibrations have the power to keep away all negativity from the environment. This was given to the great King Yudhisthira by his grandsire, Bhishma, who was a great sage. When Yudhisthira asked him, "How can I find a joy which will never leave me and satisfy my deepest desires?" Bhishma gave him the *Vishnu Sahasra Nama,* the thousand and one names of Vishnu, which has a purifying and transforming influence and fills the heart with joy. By chanting this, anger will turn to compassion, greed to generosity, and lust to love. Each of these names carries a deep significance and a continuous repetition of the names will fill the heart of both the chanter and the listener with joy.

Shiva the Destroyer

Next we come to Shiva—the destructive aspect of reality. There can be no creation without a corresponding destruction. The universe keeps constructing and destroying itself. Every cell in our body has to die and be replaced by a new one if life is to go on. The same applies to the universe. Even the planets have a span of life; our sun also will burn itself out one day. Destruction is an important and inevitable part of creation. The character of Shiva thus shows the great knowledge the rishis had about the nature of the universe. The characters of the gods are all based on scientific facts.

Shiva is the most enigmatic and most compassionate of all the gods. His form invokes fear and sometimes disgust: he is covered in ashes taken from the burning ghats (where bodies are cremated), has reptiles crawling over him, and has unkempt hair and strange-looking clothes made of animal skins. His followers are a set of fierce and odd-looking creatures, like ghouls, ghosts, dwarfs, misshapen creatures, the poor, the lowly, the despised, and the shunned. This is why he is called the most compassionate. All the creatures that others shun and despise, all the creatures that people fear and run away from in terror, all those that arouse revulsion and loathing in people, these are the ones which are loved by Mahadeva (the Great Lord). There is none so poor or hateful that is shunned by Shiva. He loves all indiscriminately since they are all creations of the Supreme.

Though he is always seen with the ugly and the dirty, yet Shiva is described as *satyam, shivam, sundaram*—the source of all truth, auspiciousness, and beauty. This contradiction found in his form is part of his nature and a part of all Nature in which beauty and ugliness are found side by side. However, when we see his true nature and open ourselves to this source of glory, it pours into our life. In order for this to happen, we have to remove the negativities within ourselves—anger, greed, lust, and ego.

Shiva's devotees abounded in south India in the twelfth century. They cared nothing for public opinion but only knew how to love God (Shiva) with the utmost devotion. They allowed allegiance to none except Shiva and no one was allowed to come in the way of their love for him. He in turn tested them to the utmost, but of course always saved them from all peril.

The worship of Shiva is closely connected with the worship of Shakti or the Divine Mother, who represents the female Energy of the universe. She is given many forms in the Puranas. Each of the gods has his own Shakti or power. Parvati is connected with Shiva as his consort. They are supposed to be eternal lovers and are very often depicted in temple sculptures bound together in a passionate embrace. Unlike Semitic religions, Hinduism never suppressed sense pleasures, because the body was always considered as the temple of the soul. The method of overcoming the lower nature is not through suppression but through sublimation. The analogy of the union between male and female is given as an example of the divine experience of bliss. The Upanishad says:

> As a man when in the embrace of a beloved wife knows nothing within or without, so the person in the embrace of the Spirit knows nothing within or without.

In Shaivism, Shiva stands for the Supreme Brahman and Parvati for Shakti or the creative force of Brahman. They signify opposite poles, both of which are absolutely necessary for all creation. This is pictorially represented in the famous form of Ardhanareesvara in which Shiva is the left side of the figure and Parvati the right side. Shakti/Parvati is the force that emanates spontaneously from the Supreme. Pure energy in any form is dangerous when not controlled. In Shaivism, Shiva controls and conditions Shakti. He is depicted as having three eyes. Shiva's two eyes, like ours, can only see duality. When he keeps them open, the world continues to exist. His third eye, on the other hand, can only experience unity, so when he opens his third eye, the cosmos, which can exist only in duality, returns to the plenum from which it was projected. As long as Shiva's third eye is open, nothing can exist. There is only *pralaya* or the undifferentiated consciousness of Absolute Reality. When he closes his third eye, Shiva comes under the sway of duality and his Shakti comes to the forefront and the cosmos rises up. The sound of *Aum* is said to be the initiating sound that causes the universe of forms.

The figure of the dancing Shiva or Nataraja is closely connected with the theories of modern quantum physics. The pioneers of modern physics were astonished when they started going into the heart of matter. At its most elemental stage, matter could not be chopped up into self-contained units or atoms. The more they delved into the core of matter, the more they were fascinated by the strange, bizarre dance of the energy particles, which were totally unpredictable. Now let us look at the famous dance of Shiva Nataraja, with his whirling locks and flailing arms. Modern photographic techniques have been able to project the lines emanating from Shiva's dancing figure and have shown that this dance actually shows the extraordinary ballet of the elementary particles as seen by the physicist.

Shiva and Parvati's eldest son is known as Ganesha and he has an elephant's head. This has an esoteric meaning. *Aum* written in Sanskrit resembles the head of an elephant with an upraised trunk. Thus, Ganesha is *pranava svaroopa* (form of *Aum*). In the alphabet of forms devised by the rishis, Ganesha comes first. He represents the foremost initiating power of the Supreme at every stage of evolution. His elephant head also exemplifies the enlightened person who can discriminate truth from falsehood, ultimate truth from unreality. His trunk is capable of lifting up big logs but it can also pick up a small pin from the ground. His position at the *muladhara chakra* or base of our spine denotes the power of gravity, which holds us down to the earth. Similarly, each one of our gods hides great scientific truths behind their extraordinary appearances.

Shiva and Parvati's second son is Kartikeya who is variously known as Subramania, Muruga, and so on. The story of Kartikeya is again the story of creation. He was born from the seed of Shiva, which was ejected into the etheric sphere and carried by Vayu or the wind to Agni or fire, who dropped it into the water, who took it and deposited it into the earth. Thus, the five elements of ether, air, fire, water, and earth combined to nurture this child of Shiva—the Supreme. Two great forces in Nature are gravity and electromagnetism. If Ganesha represents the force of gravity, Kartikeya represents electromagnetism. His *vel* or spear is an integral part of his form and is a most powerful weapon, which glints when turned here and there, sending out currents and magnetic waves. We experience the dualities of light and dark, positive and negative as a result of the electromagnetic forces that issue from Karitkeya's *vel*. The worshipper of Kartikeya is capable of controlling these waves. Masters can decode the waves and see pictures or hear sounds without the necessity of using a TV screen or recorder.

THE MEANING OF MYTHS

Though the Puranas are not really myths, the subject of myths should be discussed in this chapter, since they contain many stories that are found in other cultures and religions. Opinions differ as to what exactly the term *myth* means. A myth is a broad truth in regard to an event or a set of beings, men, animals, or others, the factual dimensions of which have either been blurred or weeded out by time as irrelevant, and which survives in people's minds, texts, memory, or traditions. In its essence a myth is truth's timeless pith, a mystique or philosophy, and the fiction amassed around it. Strangely, a myth is a truth but the term *myth* usually implies "not truth."

Ancient traditions the world over, not merely those from the realm of religion but also history, metaphysics, cosmology, medicines, and sciences, are largely myths, sometimes quite strange and unbelievable, filled with events with no apparent cause-and-effect or reciprocity, and beings beyond human conception. Many mythical traditions—such as Hindu, Christian, and Islamic—have similar myths, such as that of a great deluge submerging the earth and enveloping the entire cosmos with impenetrable darkness. They speak of a single human couple—progenitors of the human race. In many early civilizations, the myths that explore the evolution of the earth and human race have many parallels and a strange unity in their themes. They all have similar interwoven events, mystic dimensions, and a bizarre appearance. They cannot be termed as mere fiction or creations of fancy. The worldwide unanimity of these traditions suggests that the event the myth portrays, or at least its core, might have been once a reality, which, being strange and rare, gathered around it a certain amount of divinity and mysticism. It was thus mythicized and redefined or rather recycled in terms of a prevalent theology to promote its dogmatic ends, or a human value.

QUANTUM SCIENTIST RISHIS

The so-called myths of the Puranas actually contain deep scientific truths. These truths are not the facts Western science considered as truth before the twentieth century; rather, they are truths discovered by the twentieth-century quantum physicists. They are quite incomprehensible even to the modern mind, which has been slowly educated to grasp them; they would have been much more incomprehensible to people of the Puranic age. The rishis, however, as we have seen, were really superhuman, multisensory beings. They realized that these scientific facts, however true, would be quite inconceivable to the normal human being. So they wove stories round them so that people would appreciate the story even if they did not understand what it was all about. Perhaps they hoped that one day a race of *Homo sapiens* would be born who would be able to decipher their mystical language. We are fortunate to be living in this age where we can at least have a glimpse of their mighty intellect and be able to appreciate these facts since we have already learned about them from modern science.

Let us examine one of their tales, which has been totally misinterpreted. The story goes that before the creation of human beings, Brahma the Creator made himself into two—the male was Manu and the female Shatarupa. This story shows how the neutron (Brahma) was split into the proton (Manu) and the electron (Shatarupa). The bigger one was the proton and the smaller was the electron. The Upanishad goes on to say that these two particles interplayed and produced the whole universe. The scientist knows that when an electron is trapped by a proton, the former revolves round the latter and an atom of hydrogen is formed. This hydrogen atom is the primary element and is the building block of further development.

With reference to our solar system, the scriptures clearly say that our earth and all the other planets of our system originated from the sun. The fact that the earth is round was also mentioned long before Western science discovered it. In fact the rishis said that all the stars, planets, and space itself are round in shape. The Vedic seers definitely knew that the earth and other planets revolved round the sun. The hardening of the crust of the earth and its molten interior were also mentioned in the scriptures.

They also knew of the existence of galaxies and supergalaxies. *Brahamanda* is a supergalaxy. Inside the brahamanda in which we live there are fourteen *lokas* or galaxies. The loka or galaxy in which we are situated is known as *bhuh*. The other lokas situated above us are *bhuvah, svah, mahah, jana, tapa,* and *satya*. These are all mentioned in the Gayatri Mantra, by chanting which we are empowered with the energy of all these lokas. That is why the Gayatri Mantra is said to be the greatest of all the Vedic mantras. This mantra also extracts the force and energy of the sun, which is the center of our bhuh loka or galaxy. The rishis realized that the energy of the sun not only nourishes all life in this universe but also emanates certain spiritual vibrations that can be utilized by the human being in the journey to divinity. There are also seven lokas below us, known as *atala, vitala, sutala, rasatala, talatala, mahatala,* and *patala*.

In the *Devi Purana,* which contains the extraordinary stories of the Cosmic Mother or Devi, she takes the three gods of this loka or galaxy (Brahma, Vishnu, and Shiva) in her cosmic vehicle and asks them to view all the worlds that they pass. As they pass each loka or galaxy, the trinity find, to their astonishment, that each of them contains a Brahma, Vishnu, and Shiva. The goddess smilingly tells them that this is only one of the supergalaxies or brahamandas that are contained within her. From this and other stories we can see that the rishis were well aware of the infinite number of galaxies and supergalaxies, discovered only recently by Western science.

They also knew of the expanding universe. The story of Vishnu in his avatara as Vamana or the dwarf is one of the stories that depict this. Vishnu comes as a dwarf boy and begs the king of the land for a piece of land three steps long (he had come to put an end to the king's great ego). The king pities him for his stupidity and tells him to ask for the whole world if he wants since he is capable of giving him anything he asks for. But Vamana insists that he wants only three steps of land. The king agrees and Vamana takes on his cosmic form and measures the entire galaxy with one step. In his next step, he measures the whole of the brahamanda or supergalaxy. His big toe is supposed to have made a hole in this brahamanda and continued to stretch further. This is a graphic picture of the expanding universe. It shows that there is no limit to the power of God and his step can exceed even this supergalaxy and go further into unlimited space!

> *The mind is spontaneously liberated when its bondage*
> *with the visible world, its objects, events, and thoughts,*
> *is terminated. It enters the realm of pure awareness free*
> *from the memory of the past and unconcerned about the*
> *uncertainties of the future.*
>
> YOGA VASISHTA

> *The divine poet,*
> *Holding the sweet melodious flute,*
> *Reposing on the raging waves of the sea,*
> *Swiftly glides over the endless canopy of the sky.*
>
> SAMA VEDA

Loka Samasthath Sukhino Bhavantu!

ॐ

Purushottamaaya Namaha!
Salutations to the Supreme Person!

6

Bhakti

The Science of Devotion

*By contemplation on the ananda (bliss) aspect of the
Supreme as in the case of a devotee, the yogi becomes
aware of the bliss which pervades the manifested worlds.*

SHIVA SUTRA

*The mind is nothing but a derivative and differentiated
form of centralized pure consciousness and essentially of
the same nature as that consciousness.*

PATANJALI, *YOGA SUTRAS*

The human being is not only a head but also a heart that yearns for
loving fulfillment. The path of devotion called *bhakti marga* is given
to satisfy this craving of the heart. Love always asks for a reciprocal
approach and, even in devotion, which is love for God, we ask for some

response from God. Vyasa wrote the Puranas in order to meet this basic need in the human being. That is why so many gods appear in the Puranas, even though they all point and postulate the one Brahman or Paramatma—the Supreme Soul.

In the *Ramayana,* the question is asked, "Who is the Veda Vedya or the one who has to be known through a study of the Vedas?" The question was answered, "When the Supreme Being, who has to be known through the Vedas, took birth in this world, he came in the form of Rama, the son of Dasaratha." In the *Bhagavad Gita,* Lord Krishna says, *vedaischa sarvai ahameva vedyaha*—"In all the Vedas I am the only one to be known." Similarly, all the great gods of the Hindu faith identify themselves with the Supreme Being and claim no separate existence for themselves. Thus, we find that whenever any of the gods are extolled in the Puranas, most of the adjectives used for them can also be applied to Brahman.

In the twelfth chapter of the *Bhagavad Gita,* Arjuna asks a pertinent question regarding which is preferable, "Worship of God with form or worship of the formless, immutable Brahman?" Lord Krishna gives a very appropriate answer. He replies that both are equally good and will lead to the same goal of liberation but that worship of God with form is better for human beings, who are generally incapable of conceiving that which is nameless and formless. One with supreme vision is capable of seeing the same God in both the manifest and in the unmanifest. As such a vision is very rare, Hinduism offers many gods (thirty-three million are postulated) out of which any one can be chosen depending on our personality and delectation. Krishna says in the *Bhagavad Gita:*

> In howsoever a way a person approaches me, I will go to him in that very same form, for people approach me in many ways O Arjuna!

What a truly noble statement to make. Whether you approach him as Christ, Allah, Jehovah, or Krishna, it matters not, for the same force is in all and that one force or energy or spirit will approach you in that very form that appeals to you most and fulfill your desires! However, this should not be taken to mean that Hinduism considers all religions to be the same. If a devotee does not realize that the form of Christ or Allah is not confined to that particular form but actually points to the Supreme Brahman, then his or her devotion can lead to fundamentalism. It is very easy to fall into the misconception that the form we worship is the best one if not the only one!

Hence, Hinduism always insists that knowledge should precede devotion. One should understand the nature of the Supreme in its essence before starting the worship of the form. The idol is only a symbol that appeals to us. Like a signpost on a road, it points to the place we want to reach: the Infinite, formless One of the Upanishads. When a person clings to one form alone and does not realize that it is only a pointer to the Supreme, he is like a person who clings to the signpost thinking that he has reached his destination. Mistaking the signpost for the goal is what leads to all the trouble.

Only after gaining knowledge of the Supreme do we have the freedom to worship whatever form appeals to us; then we will be on the right path. The Puranas say:

Akaashath patitam toyam yada gachati sagaraath, sarva deva namaskaram keshavam pratigachati.
Just as all the water that falls from the heavens reaches the ocean, so worship of any God reaches the Supreme.

Just imagine the height of this knowledge and compassion that encompasses everything in its infinitely loving arms. This is why Hinduism never tried to convert anyone, since it considered that all paths would eventually reach the same goal. The truth is that there is only one goal even though the seekers of different faiths do not realize this.

Vyasa painted glorious word pictures in the Puranas in order to give ample scope for the devotee to soak herself in the stories of the

Divine Beloved, in whatever form her heart depicts him. It is said that even after writing the *Mahabharata* and many Puranas, Vyasa was sunk in gloom and could find no peace of mind. The Sage Narada came to him and told him that the reason for his restlessness was that he had not written the glorious tales of the great avataras of Vishnu, especially of his avatara as Krishna. It was then that he wrote the *Srimad Bhagavad Purana,* which describes all the incarnations of Vishnu, culminating in his famous role as Krishna. This is a book that ignites devotion even in those with hearts of stone. After writing it, Vyasa also found peace.

THE KITTEN PATH

The feeble instrument of the human mind lodged in this frail body finds it impossible to comprehend the loftiness of God's impersonality. We are proud of our personalities, and no stretch of imagination can reveal the meaning of utter impersonality. Because of this, devotees of the impersonal Brahman reach their goal only by imposing a tight rein on their inherent natures and using methods of constant suffering and repression. The impersonal Brahman neither accepts nor rejects their overtures, nor offers any assistance to those that clamber up in this painful manner. But it is a misunderstanding to think that just because it is a more difficult path, it is a better path. That is why Krishna tells Arjuna that worship of God with form is easier for embodied beings like us. Then the devotee can always approach the deity at whatever time or place and be assured of an instant answer.

In the *Bhagavad Gita,* when Krishna refers to himself in the first person singular, the reference is not only to the transcendent Brahman but also to that which is immanent as well. He is the Purushottama, Paramesvara, and Paramatma (Supreme Person, Supreme Lord, and Supreme Soul) all at once. It is to the unity of all these aspects that our devotion should be constantly directed. The Divine is capable of many roles, and all roles at the same time, since the only reason he has taken on a form is to bless his devotee in whatever role the devotee wishes to have him enact. As mentioned earlier, the Vedas labeled Brahman *sat-chit-ananda*—existence-consciousness-bliss. The aspect of Brahman as bliss is emphasized when It takes on a form.

This is the sweetness of bhakti yoga (the yoga of devotion). The devotee who clings to the Lord as her sole and only support in all aspects of her life—spiritual, material, mental, and intellectual—has perforce to be helped by him in all aspects, for she has no other recourse. This type of complete surrender is the easier path, since the entire responsibility of our lives is left in the capable hands of the Divine.

The scriptures make a distinction between the path of bhakti (devotion) and that of *jnana* (wisdom). The path of the *jnani* (person of wisdom) is said to be the "monkey path" while the path of the *bhakta* (devotee) is called the "kitten path." The baby monkey, like the jnani, has to cling on to his mother for dear life while she jumps from branch to branch. The moment he loosens his hold, he will fall to the hard ground below. The devotee, on the other hand, is like the kitten, carried by the mother cat from place to place without any exertion on his own part. Thus, the devotee believes that a total surrender of the ego is all that the Lord asks. If that is there, he will carry the devotee as easily as the mother cat carries its young!

The path of devotion has its own difficulties, for it demands nothing less than a complete submerging of our ego to our favorite deity along with constant communion every second of the day. Most of us, being highly egoistic, will find this very difficult to do. This path is said to be easier only because we can continuously call for help. Every time we fall we can cry to the Lord and he will come running to help us. One child learns to walk the hard way, running and falling many times, the other constantly clutches its mother's hand for support, and both reach the same goal. The option is ours. The devotee who casts the entire responsibility for her life on God will be helped by God at every moment.

THE METHODOLOGY OF DEVOTION

Many methods are given for promoting devotion in us and one of the easiest is *japa* or the repetition of our favorite God's name as many times as possible. *Japa yoga* is based on the science of phonetics. Names of gods are mantras, which have the propensity to conjure up the form of the deity. This is because the mantra is a sound that contains the form of the deity; something like the sound *dog* contains within it a picture of a dog! Thus, the mind that has been attuned to the form of its favorite deity keeps invoking him through a constant repetition and the sound enlivens the mind with thoughts of the deity, who becomes the person's constant companion.

According to Lord Krishna in the *Bhagavad Gita,* japa is one of the easiest and best methods of keeping in touch with our *ishta deva* (favorite deity). The mantra is a spiritually charged word and when we plug our mind into it, we receive the divine current directly even without our knowledge. Even a purely mechanical repetition has the power to wipe the dross of material negativity from our minds and thus allow the form to become clearer and clearer in our hearts. If even a mechanical repetition has this power, think of the power generated by someone who uses it consciously and lovingly, repeating it at all times, whatever the task she is engaged in. Bhakti yoga is indeed the yoga of love and it becomes perfect only when we begin to see God in everything around us in the world. This is when bhakti joins hands with jnana.

The devotee allows the divine will to run through her without blocking it with her personal ego. All her actions are done by the Divine and she becomes a mere instrument in his hands. This ensures that her every action is swift and sure and perfect. Combinations and calculations that are far too complicated for the normal human mind are foreseen by the Divine so no hitch occurs in any action. Every detail is looked into by her divine lover and all her wishes are foreseen. Such is the tenderness and care bestowed on her that it would be impossible to describe this state to one who has never experienced it. A personal god is the perfect lover, perfect father, and perfect mother all rolled into one. If we only have the courage to jump unhesitatingly into his arms, he will cradle us and carry us through the crocodile-infested waters of the world.

Another reason for the devotee's great feeling of security is that her beloved is always seated within her heart. Neither time nor space separates her from her beloved. He is ever present, ever loving, ever exciting, never boring—ever the perfect lover. When the heart overflows with love for the Divine, there is no place in it for love of the world. This is the secret of bhakti yoga. This may seem easier said than done. But ask any lover and he will say that he has no difficulty in keeping his mind on his beloved. Love for someone generates thoughts about that person easily and automatically. If this is so even in the mundane world, how much more will it be for the Divine? Once our minds start flowing toward God, we will find that the whole of life takes on a golden hue. The true lover has no problem in walking in the sun or rain or hail or frost so long as his beloved is with him. So also any problem of the mundane world becomes easily conquerable when one has the Divine beloved by his side. This is the glory of the path of devotion.

> *O stream of consciousness divine,*
> *These offerings are presented to you with adoration.*
> *May you acknowledge and accept our praises,*
> *And place us under your kind care,*
> *May we ever take your shelter,*
> *As a traveler takes refuge under a tree.*
>
> RIG VEDA

> *This immortal nature of the universe takes its place,*
> *In the hearts of mortal humans,*
> *And it also blesses them,*
> *In all their sacred aspirations.*

With its spiritual radiance,
Reflecting by intense love,
And knowing all secrets of wisdom,
It shines extensively.

RIG VEDA

Loka Samasthath Sukhino Bhavantu!

Sarvatjnaaya Namaha!
Salutations to the All-Knower!

7

Karma

The Science of Action

We owe a lot to the Indians who taught us how to count without which no worthwhile scientific discovery could have been made.

ALBERT EINSTEIN

It is already becoming clearer that a chapter which has a Western beginning will have to have an Indian ending if it's not to end in the self-destruction of the human race. At this supremely dangerous moment in history, the only way of salvation for mankind is the Indian way.

DR. ARNOLD TOYNBEE, BRITISH HISTORIAN

We have dealt with two great paths or yogas of Hinduism—jnana and bhakti—wisdom and devotion. Now we have to take up another of the great paths known as karma. Hinduism is the only religion that teaches us that we are totally responsible for our lives. We cannot blame God or our parents or our friends or anyone else for our problems. The law of karma is one of the foundation stones of the Sanatana Dharma and it declares categorically that our own actions are what shape our destinies. The relationship between cause and effect, which takes place between physical objects and persons, reflects a natural law that is not limited to physical reality. Everybody and everything in the physical world is part of that universal law, which we as limited human beings are not able to perceive.

We can control our actions but we cannot control the results of our actions; they are governed by the law of karma. According to this law, we receive from the world what we give to it. To put it simply, the person who hates others will keep receiving hate; the person who feels love for others will keep getting love in return. The law of karma is pretty straightforward. As we think or desire, so we shall get and become. So it is very important that we desire the right things. More than our actual actions, it is our intentions that create our future. Every intention, every desire leaves an imperceptible mark on our mind that slowly builds our future. So it is absurd to blame God for anything that happens to us. We have only ourselves to blame or praise. If we hurt others, we are actually hurting ourselves even though we may not know it. "Do to others what you would have them do to you" is a basic dictum of all religions. "As we sow, so we shall reap." This is an implacable law of Nature.

When we act, we should examine our motivation to see if it is pure or tainted with selfishness. The desire or motive with which we do an action has to be fulfilled. The fruit of that desire will come bouncing back to us one day. If some actions do not bring their results in this life, then one has to take another life in order to enjoy the benefits or be punished for the bad. Like all laws of Nature, the law of karma cannot be diverted or bypassed. This is why the Hindus believe in reincarnation, which is actually based on this scientific law of Nature.

All the laws of Nature have their corresponding components in the life of the human being. Hence, the law of karma is only a spiritual interpretation of Newton's third law of motion, which states that every action has its equal and opposite reaction. This law of motion finds its subtle expression in producing the results of the actions of the human being. If you throw a ball at a wall, it has to return to you with equal force. Similarly, if you harm someone (with intent to harm), that harm will have to return to you in some way or the other. The intention of the doer is thrown back, as it were, in an equal and opposite reaction.

Every time we act with a certain desire or with a certain intention, we are instigating a cause, which will have to end in an effect. This effect may or may not be what we expect. When it turns out to be what we expect, we are very proud of our prowess in having produced such an effect, but when it turns out to be quite different from what we expect, we tend to blame others for the way it has turned out. We are happy to accept results if they are favorable to us but not at all happy about accepting that which is undesirable or unfavorable. We totally forget that both effects have been caused by us—by our intentions, the results of which we cannot judge or gauge.

NONJUDGMENTAL JUSTICE

As a law of Nature, the law of karma has nothing to do with morality. Ethics and morality are man-made and apt to change with place and time. The law of karma, however, is an impersonal law. The universe does not judge. It is only the human being that judges. Moral rules are man-made; breaking them is an offense that has to be punished by the laws of the land. Natural laws are enforced by Nature in a totally different way.

The universal law metes out nonjudgmental justice. Therefore, according to Hinduism, this law actually serves us as an impersonal teacher of our responsibility. A person who does not understand how this law works may get angry and frustrated and start blaming God, the world, and others—anyone except himself—for how he is being treated. By doing this the person is actually creating more negative karmas for himself. In order to become liberated, each person has to balance his or her karmic debts in this life. Otherwise the imbalance will be carried on to another life like an unfinished account book in which the balance is carried over from year to year. Most accountants try to balance their books at the end of every financial year so as not to carry over certain debts. Similarly, we also should make an attempt to finish off our debts in this life. This can be done only when we realize that everything that happens to us has been created by our own intentions, either of the immediate past life or some previous ones.

We might meet many different types of personalities during the course of our life, some supportive, some hostile, some loving, some suspicious and unlikeable. If we do not want to acquire more karma, we should not judge any of their actions. Any experience we have, good or bad, is only the effect of some cause we have started at some other time, perhaps in some other lifetime. If we accept the experience without judgment, that particular cycle of cause and effect will be finished in this life, but if we react, we will be starting another cycle, the effect of which will have to be experienced by us at some other time in this life or some other life.

Of course we will recognize negativity when we see it, but we should not judge it. Judging is not our business. When we judge we create negative karma. Judgment is an action of the personality, never of the Self. Nature does not judge. God is an impersonal witness of the actions of the human being and will not interfere unless called upon to do so. To blame him for our negative experiences is a waste of time.

When we see a beggar we can be certain that he is experiencing the effect of a cause he has instigated in a previous life. Probably he refused charity to someone who was desperately in need of it and now a compassionate Nature is giving him a chance to be on the receiving end and thus balance his debts. Of course this does not mean that you should not help him. Your duty if you have the money and the means is to help him to your fullest capacity. It is not your duty to judge his worth or otherwise. If you refuse to help him, you will be starting another cycle of cause and effect, which you will have to experience. Instead of trying to balance the pros and cons yourself, all you have to do is to help the beggar if you have the means to do it without questioning his worth or his past karma. That is not your problem. Your problem is to make sure that you do not intake more negative karma by refusing to help a person who appears to be in need. Whether or not he actually deserves to be helped is not your problem.

Naturally, we are bound to see a selfish person as a selfish person and a murderer as a murderer, but we are not the ones to judge them. We cannot see the karmic debt that is being paid off by the selfishness and the murder. This does not mean that we should not act in the way that is appropriate to the situation. We can and must call the murderer to task and hand him over to the police, but that is all that we are called upon to do. The moment we start judging him from the human point of view, we become involved in the process of cause and effect. In every situation you can either look at it from the angle of your higher Self or your personality, your lower human self.

Gandhiji was beaten several times during his life. Although on two occasions he nearly died, he refused to prosecute his attackers because he saw that they were doing what they thought was right. Even when his assassinator, Godse, pointed the gun point blank at his heart, he must have held no grudge since all he did was to fold his palms in salutation and repeat "Ram, Ram!" Actually, even a good judge should meet out nonjudgmental justice. Going purely by what the jury says, he should pass his judgment without trying to judge for himself. Nonjudgmental justice allows us a great deal of freedom. Most of us go through life taking on the task of judging others and thus creating a lot of negative karmas for ourselves. A knowledge of the law of karma allows us to go our own way without judging but nevertheless doing what we are called upon to do. We can rest assured that nothing escapes this law, which is all-pervasive, so everyone will get his or her just desserts without our interference.

MAINTAINING BALANCE

Every relationship that we have with anyone, however trivial, has a karmic basis. In order to progress spiritually, the individual has to balance his karmic debts. He has to experience the effects that he has caused either in this life or in another. All our relationships are given to us in order to balance some debt or other. This applies to other parties also. But of course, how they choose to heal themselves is their problem, whereas our problem is somehow to pay our debts as fast as possible without incurring more karmic debts.

Whether we will finish off our karmic bond with our debts in this life will depend on whether we react or respond to the stimuli we receive from them. Like, dislike, and indifference are the three types of responses we normally have to anything and anyone. All these might cause further karmic bonds if they are not called for. Even if our dislike or indifference has a cause, we should not react with a similar feeling. The only way to negate the cycle of cause and effect is to accept. We have to learn to accept the person as he or she is without trying to project our own likes or dislikes on him or her.

The universe does not like to leave anything incomplete. Every cause has to produce an effect. Until it does so, the circle is incomplete. Sometimes it happens that this balancing of energy may not take place in this lifetime. Therefore, the embodied soul has to take on another form in order to complete the process. The effects of my actions have to be experienced by me and not by anyone else. If I die before I experience them, I will be compelled to take on another body so as to complete the process. The jivatma (embodied soul) takes a new birth, carrying what is known as his or her *prarabdha karma,* all the actions which it has started or caused in a previous life. The effects of these have to be experienced by the jivatma. But the jivatma can keep from instigating new karmas, which are the causative factors for new effects in the future.

If, in this life, I find that I'm repeatedly being treated cruelly by others, I might strike back and treat others as they have been treating me (tit for tat). However, if I understand the law of karma I will realize that I must have treated many people cruelly in my previous life and now I'm being given an opportunity to balance the effects of my past karma by having many people treat me cruelly. If I understand this and accept this without hatred for those who do injustice to me, then I will have washed off that karma from my plate and can start my next life with a clean conscience.

Every experience we have in this life, whether good or bad, is actually the means employed by a compassionate universe to enable us to balance our debts and start afresh. The way we accept our lives will pave the way for our future lives. If we lash out with pain and hatred at those who revile us, we might have balanced one karmic debt, but we will be starting another one. If, however, we accept what happens without rancor and without reacting, we will be nullifying the effects of that particular karma and will be able to end that cycle of cause and effect. This is beautifully explained by Lord Krishna in the *Srimad Bhagavad Gita*. The jivatma takes on a physical reality in order to balance its karmas within the framework of the law of karma. We can only evolve as individuals, groups, and societies within this framework.

Anyone who performs actions only for himself without any care or consideration for others and for the world around him will have to suffer. This is the law of Nature. Any selfish act immediately isolates us from the world and from Nature; many such acts eventually bring unhappiness, discontent, ill health, and continuous bad luck, which we blame on others and on our fate, never realizing that it is only a consequence of our own selfish actions. Here is where the law of karma comes into play. Our world is shaped by our own actions. In this respect we must understand that our thoughts are also actions. As Krishna says, in the human being, motivation is even more important than the actual action. A violent act may do some good to the person concerned, like a surgeon cutting off a gangrenous hand in order to save the patient's life, but when the hand is cut off by a thief who wants to steal the golden bangle on it, then the same action is violent and violates the law of Nature; it thus brings its own violent consequences to the doer. This is the very basis of the law of karma.

VEDIC GUIDEBOOK

How can we be held responsible for our actions if we do not know how to act? This is why the Vedas give so many details about behavior and action. The different sections present certain patterns of behavior that should be practiced by all sections of society in order to know the Infinite Being. In and through all the rituals and codes of conduct mentioned in the Vedas, one fact is reiterated: all are done in order to know That. We should practice certain mental disciplines in order to keep the thought of that Being steady before us. The performances of sacrifices, of doing penance, giving charity, going to temples, social service, marriage rites, and all such duties are meant only to give us mental purity (*chitta shuddhi*) and to steady the wavering mind (*chitta vritti nirodha*). The object of all the various duties and acts enjoined on us in the Vedas is to help realize that Brahman through a disciplined path.

Instead of letting the sense organs and mind drag us where they will, we should perform the prescribed Vedic and Puranic rituals by which we will be able to develop the capacity to see inwardly. The intellect is actually capable of grasping everything and can reach That, by knowing which all things will become known. However, to do this, it has to analyze and find out and eliminate all those things that are not necessary for its progress. Attachment to the body increases by performing impure acts and leads to loss of mental peace. But the repetition of the Vedic mantras and observing the rituals given in the Puranas, which are designed to bring universal well-being, will lead us to spiritual maturity and allow us to gain moksha or liberation.

The self-realized soul transcends time and space and
abides in pure consciousness. No evil thoughts, desires, or
fear can ever enter his enlightened mind.

ASHTAVAKRA GITA

The cosmic pair of day and night,
Come to cherish our noble deeds,
Like two deer in a forest,
Like two wild cattle on fresh pastures,
Like two swans flying in the sky.

RIG VEDA

Loka Samasthath Sukhino Bhavantu!

Anaghaaya Namaha!
Salutations to the Flawless One!

8

The World of Maya
Reality Is Not What We Think It Is

*All matter originates and exists only by virtue of a force
which brings the particles of an atom to vibration and
holds this minute solar system of the atom together. We
must assume behind the force the existence of a conscious
and intelligent mind. This mind is the matrix of all
matter.*

MAX PLANCK

*You are neither earth, nor air, nor sky, but you live
happily in all these things. You are pure intelligence that
creates and witnesses the drama of existence.*

ASHTAVAKRA GITA

*Who knows your true reality?
You take birth though unborn,*

You destroy evil though without movement,
You are asleep though ever wakeful.

RAGHUVAMSA BY KALIDASA

Maya is a word that is very familiar to the Western world and is often used quite glibly, but very few actually know what it means. It was first used in the Advaita Vedanta school of Hinduism to describe this universe of changing forms. The original meaning of *maya* was the magical creative power of Brahman. Its meaning has changed over the centuries. From the might or power of the Divine Magician, it has also come to signify the psychological state of anybody under the spell of the magic show. When we confuse the myriad forms of the divine play with reality, without perceiving the unity of Brahman underlying these forms, we are under the spell of maya. Maya is like a well-dressed, heavily made-up woman who appears beautiful and enticing. It is only when her makeup is removed that her real form can be seen. Maya is not illusion but that which creates some sort of delusion in us, which makes us think that the shapes and forms and events in which we live are real. It is the power of confusing concepts for reality, of confusing the map with the territory!

In Hinduism, *maya* is described as a state of "becoming." The Puranas describe it poetically. Shiva in his form as the Absolute is called Bhava or "Being," whereas Parvati who is the essence of maya is known as Bhavani or "Becoming." There can be no change or activity without expenditure of energy. The Sanskrit word for energy is *shakti*. Hinduism, with its genius for personification, says that Shakti is a feminine principle of Brahman, which is coexistent with it. Out of this feminine principle of Shakti, countless goddesses have been created by the prolific minds of the rishis. Thus, every god is given his own Shakti—Shiva/Parvati, Lakshmi/Narayana, Brahma/Sarasvati, and so on. Scientific facts are neatly interwoven into the Puranic stories.

Maya/Shakti projects this dynamic world. It is only by stripping her of her external accoutrements that we can expose the Reality that is her support. She is not an existent reality and has no existence apart from Brahman. Hence, the rishis said that the world is maya. Even though it appears to be solid and real, it is actually not what we think it is. Thus another meaning for the word *maya* is *yama*—"that which doesn't exist." So if this world is maya, it would follow that it is something that does not exist.

Our rishis have been telling us for centuries that reality is not what we think it is. It is a kind of play or passing show. Then, with the dawn of the twentieth century, modern physics started to support this view wholeheartedly. The greatest thing that quantum physics did for the spiritually minded person was to show that the world of the senses is not a solid thing, as Newtonian physics had claimed.

Sir Isaac Newton, said to be the father of classical physics, was deeply impressed by the mechanistic view of the universe as given by Descartes. This view dominated all scientific thought from the second half of the seventeenth century to the end of the nineteenth century. Newton believed that the world was created by God, who assembled all the different objects and made a huge machine. In devising the world machine, God created the material particles, the forces between them, and the fundamental laws of motion. Creation took place one fine day and God breathed into this machine the first impulse so that it would run; since then the world machine keeps running on immutable laws like a gigantic clock. All natural laws are invariable and eternal. God transcends the world and rules it from above. The Newtonian world was a lonely place in which the human being had no place. The world carried on whether we were present or not, almost as if we are mere witnesses to a show that goes on with or without our participation. This made man into a mere cog in a machine.

With one squiggle of his pen, Einstein exploded the deterministic, mechanical view of matter. A revolution occurred in the thought of Western scientists—a battle between accepted beliefs and empirical truth as provided by the scientist. This is what early-twentieth-century astrophysicist Arthur Eddington said about the world:

> The world that we experience in everyday life is a convenient mirage attuned to our very limited sense—an illusion conjured by our perceptions and our mind. All that is around us (including our own bodies) which appears so substantial is ultimately nothing but ephemeral networks of particles and waves whirling round at lightning speed, colliding, rebounding, disintegrating in almost total emptiness. So-called matter is mostly emptiness, proportionately as void as galactic space, void of anything except occasional dots and spots of scattered electric charges.

These physicists went to the heart of matter and were astounded by what they saw. Matter was not solid at all but merely energy in motion. In fact, matter is composed of subatomic particles that have no design or shape and do not follow any standard order. Sometimes they behave like waves and sometimes like particles and sometimes they are both at the same time. Hence, these physicists actually proved the maya theory in a scientific way.

GOING BEYOND QUANTUM PHYSICS WITH SHANKARA

Adi Shankaracharya, founder of the Advaita Vedanta school of Indian philosophy taken from the Upanishads, describes the cognition of the illusory world in a way that is very close to what the quantum physicist says:

> Its form cannot be determined with any degree of certainty. It is apparent like a dream, water, or a mirage. It is fugitive, its own form being evinced and not evinced. Therefore it has no end, no fixity, and no determinacy and never stays as a particular form, exclusive of other forms. It can never be determined conclusively.

Heisenberg's principle of indeterminacy (the uncertainty principle) repeats this in modern language. Heisenberg says that it is impossible to determine with absolute precision both the position and the momentum of a particle simultaneously. When the position of the particle is determined with accuracy, its velocity is automatically altered. Consequently, the momentum of the particle is changed. As a result the value of the momentum of the particle becomes uncertain at the time of the accurate determination of its position. The more accurate the determination of one, the greater the uncertainty of the other. We can only approximately know the position and the momentum of the particle simultaneously. The more we know about one, the less we know about the other. When we know the one with absolute precision, we know nothing whatsoever about the other! How close this is to Shankara's assertion made more than two thousand years ago.

Shankara, being a great spiritualist, went one step further in describing the nature of the illusory world. He said that the human mind very cleverly superimposes reality on the unreal. The classic example he gives of this is the rope and the snake. In the darkness of the night one might imagine a snake to be lying at the side of a room. When a light is brought or turned on it will reveal that the snake is actually a coiled-up rope. Here the unreal is superimposed on the real. The snake cannot be considered as real because once knowledge is obtained with the aid of the light, the snake disappears. It cannot be totally unreal either, since for all practical purposes it did exist for the viewer for a short while, causing fear, palpitation, and all the other side effects. Shankara goes on to say that we have created this world in a similar manner, superimposing a false reality on external objects.

Again and again all our scriptures say that this world that we think of as real is only maya or an appearance. It is only a passing show with no permanent reality. The experiments related to atomic events have revealed that the elementary particles form a world of potentialities or possibilities rather than one of actual facts. These subatomic particles have no objective existence. They are not like particles of dust. Thus Heisenberg concludes:

> Elementary particles are not real as objects of daily life, like stones and sticks. In spite of all our attempts in the search for the ultimate stuff of the universe, we finally have come to the conclusion that there is nothing like that!

The theory of relativity shows that we can observe only relations, while the quantum theory says that we can observe only probabilities. Together they have come to the conclusion that the mathematical equations that pertain to particles of wave packets in their different states do not actually represent them in actual fact. They merely indicate the different kinds of knowledge we can have about them. Therefore, modern science has given up all claims to be specific. It deals with the grounds of possible knowledge and not with the essence of a fundamental reality.

CONSCIOUSNESS IS KEY

Advaita Vedanta declares that the universe is an illusion created by the participators in this drama. The Copenhagen interpretation of quantum mechanics is in complete agreement with this. It says that the world we perceive as a physical reality is actually our mental construction of it. Although this mental construction appears to be solid, the physical world itself is not. They did not take the weak stand that the physical world as we see it "may or may not" exist but declared categorically that it "does not" exist as we see it.

The question can then be raised as to how the Supreme unchangeable substance turned into the changing world. Vedanta describes this unique phenomenon by postulating maya as the cause of the superimposition. Maya has two powers, one to veil and the other to project. It veils Brahman and projects pluralities on the nondual. How is this done? Let us take the example of light and darkness. Light exists, darkness does not. The latter is only the absence of the former. Although darkness does not exist in reality, it has empirical existence. Similarly, Adi Shankara and other Vedantins recognized the empirical existence of the world. Even though all the things seen in a magic show are not real, yet they have a sequence and are meaningful to the spectators. In our relative and dependent existence, anything that has a relative existence cannot be ignored.

The quantum world sharpens into concrete reality when an observation is made. In the absence of an observer, the atomic world is only a possibility. The particles materialize only when we look for them. When you look for the location of a particle you can find it at a particular place but you cannot gauge its speed. When you want to gauge its speed, it becomes a wave and you can see it in motion. However, you cannot fix both its location and speed at the same time. So-called reality displays itself only when there is an observer and cannot be separated from him. Quantum physics prefers the word *participator* to *observer*. We cannot observe a thing without influencing it and in reality we are actually creating our world. A particle with momentum did not exist before the experimenter conducted an experiment to measure its position. Thus, the modern-day physicists say that particles have "a tendency to exist" and not that they really exist.

Thus, the quantum physicist discovered something novel, which the ancient physicist could not accept—that the only thing that can be called real in this shadow world is the consciousness of the spectator or the experimenter. Without that consciousness, even this shadow world would not exist. Everything is centered around the experimenter. This was a great breakthrough. Till then the experimenter's job was always to get out of the way of the experiment and not interfere with the purely mechanical process involved in the experiment. Then the scientists came to understand that the individual consciousness has everything to do with the final outcome of the experiment.

Normally quantum particles act in a haphazard fashion of chaos or disorder but when the individual consciousness is brought to bear on them, they lose their individuality and begin to act as a single unit. The vital thing here is the intrinsic *participation* of the observer. John Wheeler says:

Is it possible that the universe in some strange sense is brought into being by the participation of those who participate?

Classical theory says the observer is the one who stands safely behind a glass wall and watches what goes on without participating in anything. This is an impossibility according to quantum physics. Thus, the quantum physicist corroborates the claim of the rishis that the world exists only because we, the observers, are actively participating in it. The world is a creation of the human mind. Each of us creates our own world. These words are used by both Vedanta and by the quantum physicists.

In the conscious state we experience a reality created by the processing of sensory information relayed by the nerves to the brain. Memory and emotions can modify these inputs in order to create separate aspects of the external world. But all these neural activities are of no use without some type of consciousness that integrates all these experiences into a coherent whole. Without consciousness, we cannot experience existence. It is because of consciousness that our brain has meaningful experiences both of the external world as well as the internal world of feelings and emotions.

This is where religion and especially Hindu spiritualism steps in to show us that some things exist that are beyond the level of the mind. Normally, quantum particles act in a haphazard fashion of chaos or disorder but when the individual consciousness is brought to bear on them, they lose their individuality and begin to act as a single unit. This coherence extends into the world. This coherence of consciousness represents the greatest form of order known to Nature and can help to shape and create order in the world.

CHITTA AND THE ZERO POINT FIELD

The zero point field is the most fundamental state of matter. It is a heaving sea of energy—one vast quantum field. On the quantum level, all living beings including human beings are packets of quantum energy, which are constantly exchanging information with the inexhaustible field of energy, known as *chitta* in Hindu terminology. This is the substructure that underlies the whole universe. It is a recording medium of everything, by which everything can communicate with everything else.

Information about all aspects of life is relayed through the interchange of information on the quantum level. Have you watched a flight of birds gliding their way across the sky and how suddenly all of them veer to a different course as if at some hidden signal? The same phenomenon can be noticed in schools of fish. It had been assumed that these birds and fish had a novel method of communicating with each other by some radar or noise signal that we cannot hear, but experiments have proved that they are all in touch with the quantum field and receive their orders simultaneously from it. This is the substructure that underlies the whole universe. It is a recording medium of everything, by which everything can communicate with everything else. The functions of our minds such as thinking, feeling, and so on draw information from the quantum field, which is pulsing simultaneously through our body and brain. We resonate with the universe.

Living consciousness is not an isolated entity. It is not the personal property of one individual. We think that each of us has a separate atman, but our scriptures tell us that when this apparently separate atman is covered with the body, it is called the jivatma, which is the same as the Paramatma. It lives on even after the body dies; as it has never been isolated from the whole, there is no question of going back. It simply slips into what it was, like water from a pool that is held in a bottle returning to the pool when the bottle is broken.

Our consciousness has incredible powers. In meditation and especially in the state of samadhi, our brain reaches that zero point field of the chitta, which has perfect coherence. It can increase order in the world and make it as we wish it to be. If a number of individuals concentrate and wish for the same thing, consciousness has even greater force. That is why we say that communal prayer has more power. The all-absorbing topic of the day is how to control the climatic changes that are being increasingly felt all over the world. If enough people had a burning desire to change the situation, they would do far better if they got together and meditated on this topic, willing the minds of people to change, and thus stop the terrible effects we have brought upon ourselves. This would be far more effective than holding conferences and reading papers.

Maharishi Mahesh Yogi demonstrated that a number of individuals meditating at the same time can produce a great amount of coherence in the world outside. This was also proved by physicists who conducted experiments that showed that the more people who were wishing for a certain outcome, the more likely it was to take place. Even machines are affected by our attitude. Whereas Newtonian science had totally divorced man from the universe, quantum science has demonstrated that there is a purpose and unity in life and we are an important part of it. What we do and think is critical in creating our world. We are not isolated beings living our desperate lives on a lonely planet in an indifferent universe. We are always at the center of everything. We have the power both individually and collectively to heal ourselves and improve our own lives and the lives of others around us.

Human consciousness (as our scriptures have always told us) is a crucial factor in making up this universe. Since we are totally connected with everything and every creature in this universe, for each of us to strive to better ourself without regard to what happens to others is the most foolish thing that we could do. Human suffering stems from this very fact, that we have cut ourselves off from our roots and have condemned ourselves to a life of isolation. This was not how ancients wanted us to live. The greatest of the Vedic hymns keep this in view. *Loka samastha sukhino bhavantu*—"Let the whole world be happy." Despite the various attacks on her culture and constant efforts to bring her religion down, India has always stuck to this slogan—*Loka samastha sukhino bhavantu.*

NOT REAL; NOT UNREAL

At various ages of time, Western science has tried to fix reality in terms of matter, or energy, field, or space. None of these proved satisfactory. Once Einstein himself thought "the field" to be the only reality. Shortly before his death, he declared that "space" was the only reality. All attempts to fix reality on matter, energy, particles, field, and space were failures. Advaita Vedanta says that all these are products of maya and cannot be considered as real. The extreme view of the universe, as given by Shankara's teacher, Gaudapada, postulates that the universe is not real—*Brahma satyam, jagat mithya*: "Brahman alone is real, the world is unreal."

In science two laws are considered fundamental and inviolate. One is the law of conservation of matter and the other the law of conservation of energy. The first says matter is neither created nor destroyed; the sum total of matter in the universe is constant. There may be transformation of matter from one form to another. The second law says energy is neither created nor destroyed; the sum total of energy in the universe is constant. There may be transformation of energy from one form to another. The same thing was said by Lord Krishna in the *Bhagavad Gita* (chapter 11) ten thousand years before. "Existence cannot come out of nonexistence nor can nonexistence ever become existent." This is a formal law that can never be invalidated.

We recognize something as existent (*sat*) when it is perceived by our senses directly or indirectly. What is not perceptible to our senses we consider it as nonexistent (*asat*). Hence, existence and nonexistence are relative terms based on the ability or inability of our senses to perceive them. So when we say that the universe was nonexistent before creation, we mean that it was not perceivable by our senses at that time. Advaita says that the universe is always existent in a subtle form and is perceivable by the senses only when it takes on a gross form. *Avyakta* (unmanifest) and *vyakta* (manifest) are the two terms used by Vedanta to describe these subtle and gross states. According to Vedanta, creation is the manifestation or an emanation of something that existed in an unmanifest state. Therefore, the universe cannot be called either sat (existent) or asat (nonexistent). However, for us, what is manifested is sat (existent) and what is unmanifest is asat. Vedanta says that this sat is only a transient existence that is perceivable to us for a short while; it has no permanence; whereas what we think of as asat is actually something that is eternally existent but nonperceivable by our five senses.

Thus, in Vedanta even that which we think of as asat or nonexistent is actually sat or existent. This concept was first given in the "Nasadiya Sukta" of the *Rig Veda,* which says that before the universe came into being, it was neither sat nor asat. It was not sat since it could not be perceived by the senses, and it was not asat since it existed in a subtle state. Before the universe came into being, Brahman alone existed. Since the universe could not be produced out of nothing, we must conclude that it is an emanation from Brahman. As discussed earlier, the concept of Brahman as given in Advaita Vedanta is undifferentiated, homogeneous existence, functionless, timeless, unchangeable, and nonmodifiable. So how can it be the cause of the universe?

Can we then say that the universe was produced out of nothing? Vedanta does not accept this. Something cannot come out of nothing and nothing cannot become something. Vedanta does not recognize "nothingness" or void or vacuum, *shunya.* It says that everything is plenum or fullness, *poorna.*

> *Poornamadah, poornamidam.*
> *Poornat poornamudachyate.*
> *Poornasya poornamaadaya,*
> *poornamevavashishyate.*

That is full, this is also full.
Out of the full, fullness comes.
If you take away fullness from the full,
fullness alone remains.

Physics also has come to the conclusion that there is no such thing as a void. The so-called vacuum is far from being empty. It contains an unlimited number of particles that spontaneously keep coming into being and vanishing all the time. As Fritjof Capra says:

The physical vacuum is not a state of mere nothingness but contains the potentiality for all forms of the particle world. These forms in turn are not independent physical entities but merely transient manifestations of the underlying void. The relation between the virtual particles and the vacuum is dynamic. The vacuum is truly a living void, pulsating in endless rhythms of creation and destruction.

If the universe has come out of Brahman, which is ever full, then the universe also must be ever full. In other words, the universe must also be Brahman! However, Brahman cannot be divided into parts, so what we think of as parts or differences are actually a superimposition on the reality of Brahman, which is the only reality. So the universe has only an empirical reality, like a mirage on desert sands. That is why it is termed *maya*, something which actually does not exist in the form that we imagine it to be. Again this is what quantum physics says, that what we think of as solid matter (the world) is only energy in motion!

Modern physics can only tell us about this lower nature, or maya, and is not capable of telling us anything of the nature of Ultimate Reality. Eddington declared that the great difference between old and new physics is that, though both are dealing with shadow symbols, the new physics has been forced to accept the fact that it is indeed dealing with shadows—a set of abstract equations—and not with Reality itself.

As Hinduism says, we can only see maya or the power of Brahman; we can never see the underlying cause. Even though physicists are able to reduce matter to its ultimate and fundamental state and put it into mathematical equations, yet to date they have not been able to reduce God into a mathematical equation.

The Ultimate Reality that has ever existed and which will ever exist, and which alone is, can only be experienced by the sage, the seer, and the mystic who connects with the source and draws inspiration from it. As the Gita says, such a person can no longer be labeled a human being but has to be given the title of a god. The future of the world lies in the production of such god men and not in the production of more nuclear weapons.

BURSTING OF THE COSMIC EGG

From this we understand that there is one great difference between the views of modern science regarding creation and the Vedantic view. Even though science claims that the universe was created out of a big bang, it gives no cause for the explosion nor can it tell us what existed before the explosion. Scientists cannot tell us how a universe obeying all the intricate physical laws that ours does could emerge from a big explosion. From supergalaxies to the lowest form of life, everything contains matter and forces that have been created with great mathematical precision. What kind of mighty brain could have created the blueprint of this complex universe in which we are living?

Martin Rees, an expert on cosmology, gives six numbers as a recipe for our universe. They are so crucial that if any one of them had not been chosen correctly, nothing would have emerged as we see it today. In fact we would not even be here contemplating these possibilities! The first of these is 10 to the power of 36, a vital number that shows how feeble gravity is compared to the electrical forces that hold atoms together. If this were not so, gravity would have crushed everything and there would have been no question of a universe. There are five other numbers that are equally vital for the building of this complex cosmos, but we need not go into them now. Suffice to say that all these marvels which we see now could not have come about by mere chance. The random emergence of a universe with all the necessary parameters for creation is an impossibility. Rees says that all the ingredients necessary for creating this universe must have been envisaged by the initial entity that existed before the big bang.

The solution given by the Vedas is that of a superintelligent vacuum, but this is something the scientists are loathe to accept, since it is far beyond their known parameters. This leaves them with a string of coincidences, which is as irrational as accepting the grace of a superintellect. Both explanations lack experimental evidence, though the Vedic explanation of the superconsciousness of Brahman has the experiential evidence of the rishis, which again the scientist cannot accept. The mystery of the emergence of this type of an incredible creation remains unsolved in the scientific world.

The latest scientific discovery apparently is of something called a Higgs-boson particle, which is being called the "God particle" in common parlance. This is such an important find that the whole scientific world is agog, for they think that it might solve the riddle of life once and for all. But it is a very elusive particle that defies all attempts to pinpoint it to one place and time. It never stays for long in one place so proper experiments on it are very difficult. Still, the scientific world continues to hope that something will come of it. According to the *Aitareya Upanishad,* the Creator is present in all forms of life even though we cannot see it. It is as elusive as the God particle. This intelligent energy is the very essence of our existence, though it appears in varying degrees of intensity in different creatures.

The cosmogony of Advaita Vedanta is evolutionary. Shankaracharya says that the universe evolved gradually and that things did not appear suddenly in their final shapes. However, the Advaitic concept of evolution is different from the Darwinian. Darwin's theory of evolution is species oriented and not spiritually oriented. It has three phases:

inorganic, organic, and species. The evolutionary sequence given in the *Taittiriya Upanishad* also follows this pattern—inorganic, organic, and species. It describes the evolution from matter to life, life to mind, mind to intellect, and intellect to bliss. The Darwinian process is not guided by any intelligence. Vedanta, however, says that Brahman is chit or Pure Consciousness. The power or shakti of that consciousness, which is also known as maya, evolves due to the presence of that intelligence within it. Consciousness is eternal and timeless; maya is also eternal and timeless but unconscious. The presiding spirit called Isvara, who is omniscient, is also eternal and timeless. The universe does not come out of nothing nor does it become nothing. Maya, shakti, or prakriti, though insentient, is the active principle of Brahman, but remains in a dormant state until the time comes for another creation and evolution. The creation takes place under the gaze of the cosmic intelligence or Brahman. *Srishti, sthiti,* and *samhara* (creation, maintenance, and destruction) follow a cyclical pattern.

Advaita Vedanta accepts the big bang theory. Since the rishis were experts in clothing scientific truths in poetic form, this theory is expressed as the bursting of the cosmic egg. References to the cosmic egg have been given in many of the Hindu scriptures. This cosmic egg was filled with a fluid called *apah*. Many translators describe *apah* as water, but this is not so. It is a fluid whose exact nature is not known to us. The creative principle, Brahma, resided in the cosmic egg for one divine year consisting of many light years before the egg exploded and he came out and created the universe from the primordial substance of the cosmic egg. The Vedas also mention that the stars and planets were formed out of the gas clouds and dust of space that came out of the egg.

In Puranic literature, the bursting of the cosmic egg is described poetically. At the beginning of creation, Lord Narayana reposes on his serpent bed on the sea of all possibilities (the zero point field of modern physics). From his navel comes the golden lotus on which Brahma, the Creator, is seated. He brings forth the Hiranyagarbha or the golden egg, which bursts and creates the numerous worlds. In another version of the story, Lord Vishnu, who is in charge of maintaining the universe, is said to be sleeping on the cosmic waters. A golden lotus comes out of his navel and from this the cosmic egg is developed. Brahma, the Creator, is residing inside the egg. Vishnu advises Brahma to practice austerities to gain the knowledge of how to create. Through his deep meditation he disturbs the fluid in the egg which results in the bursting of the egg. The evolutionary process started with this big bang.

When the egg exploded, prana was let out. Now we think of *prana* as life or the vital force of both living and nonliving entities. Here *prana* denotes the substance that appeared after apah. Nothing in the universe can function without help from prana. The violent explosion caused prana to vibrate violently. As a result, an excessive quantity of heat was produced. In that superheated state, akasa, or space, emanated from prana. Brahma produced energy particles and matter particles in opposite pairs from akasa.

Apah, prana, and akasa are almost the same substance and differ only in their subtlety. In that superheated state after the explosion of the cosmic egg, light particles (photons) were dominant. Akasa kept producing particle pairs, which were reconverted into akasa. The Rig Veda describes this phenomenon as Daksha being born of Aditi and Aditi being born of Daksha. Aditi has been described as both the parent and the offspring since the reverse process is possible and akasa may be converted into prana. Due to her importance in creation, Aditi was revered as a goddess, the mother of all the gods or energy particles. The particles (*renu*) were dancing vigorously in the superheated condition in an extremely chaotic manner and thus there was constant collision, annihilation, and transmutation. No atoms could be formed due to the random movements of the particles. It was an energy-dominated state and there was hardly any matter except in the form of particles and antiparticles.

These three words, *apah, prana,* and *akasa,* represent the three substates of the single state known in quantum physics as "the field." The subtlest state of the field is known as apah, or primal waters. The next state is prana, and finally comes akasa. Modern science has not differentiated these three as yet. The field consisting of these three subtle states is full of activity. Particles and antiparticles are produced from it and again and again they merge back into it. The universe expands due to the expansion of the field. According to the Upanishads, gaseous matter (*vayu*) was produced from akasa. *Vayu* is commonly translated as "air" in the earth's atmosphere but at that time the earth had not come into being, so what was meant by *vayu* was gaseous matter. From akasa came vayu, the source of hydrogen, the simplest of all gases. Due to the compression of hydrogen, heat was produced and this heat liquefied the gas. These two processes have been described in the Upanishads as agni (fire) being produced from vayu (gas), and apah (liquid) being produced as a result of the heating of the gaseous matter. In the course of billions of years, the exterior parts of the planetary sphere became solidified. The word used in the scriptures for this phenomenon is *prithvi*. In the course of time, these words have come to have different meanings and refer to the *pancha bhutas* (five elements), which compose the material world: *akasa* or *vyoma* for space, from which came *vayu* or air, and then *agni* or *tejas,* which is heat energy or fire, from which came *apas* or water, and finally *prithvi* (earth) or solid matter.

According to Hinduism, creation is cyclical and not linear as in the West. Every manifestation is preceded by a period when everything is unmanifest. Before every manifestation, the universe is potentially existent in maya. So the big bang that scientists have observed is only one in a series of big bangs. All of the happenings that have been described here will take place with every big bang. At the appropriate time each creation will end its cycle of existence and revert to its causal agents, after which it will manifest once again in another big bang.

Maya has three constituents known as *gunas*: *sattva, rajas,* and *tamas.* In physics these three are known as harmony, kinesis, and inertia. The processes of creation (*srishti*), preservation (*sthiti*), and dissolution (*pralaya*) cannot take place when the three gunas of maya are in a state of equilibrium. As long as these three are in balance, creation is at rest. When the time comes for another manifestation, a ripple transmitted by Brahman appears in the still waters of maya. This vibration is in the form of a sound, *Aum*. From this first sound the whole universe of names and forms is manifested. The dormant, potential, unmanifest universe becomes manifest when rajas or the quality of kinesis comes into prominence. The preservation of the universe in its manifested state is carried on during the stage in which sattva is predominant. When tamas becomes predominant, the process of dissolution becomes operative.

Everything in the universe has these three constituents in its make-up—sometimes sattva predominates, sometimes rajas, and sometimes tamas. One follows the other and most things are a mixture of all three. Even in our own bodies and characters, these three have free play. When sattva predominates, we are calm and peaceful; when rajas predominates, we become very active; and when tamas rules, we become lazy or sleepy. Of course these three keep changing their roles constantly, hence we get the beautiful drama of life with its changing patterns, painful incidents interspersed with beautiful and serene interludes.

LIBERATION FROM MAYA

Although maya is said to be the material cause of the universe, it is insentient like wood or gold. Wood cannot be converted into a chair or table without a carpenter. The carpenter has the skill and is called the efficient cause. When we observe the world both on the micro and the macro levels, it is intelligently designed for specific purposes. It has both design and beauty. From the world of subatomic particles up to the galaxies, stars, and planetary systems, there appears to be a perfect plan. In the gross and subtle structures of both the living and nonliving world, we again see planning and design. However, the insentient star and planetary systems are totally ignorant of this.

Even the human being who is supposed to be the most intelligent animal on earth has still not been able to decipher the mystery of the universe and the amazing arrangement of the working of his own body and brain! Without his conscious effort, his own system functions purposefully and intelligently. This happens with all systems—plants, bacteria, viruses, galaxies, and so on. The materialists say this is all done "naturally." What exactly is implied by the word *naturally*? Can you take a few logs of wood, throw them in the air, and expect a chair? By a deep observation of the plan of the universe and of our own bodies and minds, any rational being will have to infer the existence of an invisible planner and designer, call It what you will.

Albert Einstein says:

> Certain it is that a conviction, akin to religious feeling, of the rationality or the intelligibility of the world lies behind all scientific work of a higher order. This firm belief, a belief bound up with deep feeling, in a superior mind that reveals itself in the world of experience, represents my conception of God.

The position of Western scientists is that of *jijnasus* or inquirers on the path of truth as the *Gita* puts it. They are eager and anxious to know the truth but somehow this ultimate truth seems to defy all attempts at generalizations. Hence, we see that even though we live in this highly scientific age, even educated people tend to believe in the occult and the miraculous. There seem to be some things in the world that defy scientific investigation.

If we realize that maya is only a veil that hides reality from us—an appearance that has been produced at some point in space and time—then we are no longer under the spell of maya. We will understand that it is only a display of forms. The only way to break free from this spell of the enchantress Maya is to come to a realization that all the phenomena we perceive with our five senses are part of the same reality. This is known as moksha or liberation. This means that we begin to personally experience that everything including our own self is nothing but Brahman. This is the very essence of Hinduism.

How do we attain this realization? Many techniques like meditation and different types of yoga are given in Hinduism, but we should also look at what the great twentieth-century sage of Thiruvannamalai, Ramana Maharishi, advised. He brought forward the Upanishadic view even more forcibly. He said that the essence of consciousness is embedded in the core of the human mind. The Upanishads already state that "atman and Brahman are equal." The true nature of consciousness is revealed to us only when maya is removed from the mind through right perception. How to remove this maya is the next question. Ramana advocated the method known as "self-inquiry" in order to remove the veil of maya. "Who am I?" is the question he asked people to use. By negating all those parts of ourselves that are transitory or superficial we will come to the realization that we are nothing other than that Supreme Consciousness of Brahman. This is indeed liberation from all the fears that haunt the mind of the human being. Fear of death and extreme attachment to people, places, and objects are banished forever with this basic knowledge, which must be made a part of our everyday life.

Our inquiry into our true selves should make us realize that the Supreme Self is equally present in all beings irrespective of any perceived differences. Meditation and different types of yoga can only give us occasional glimpses of the Supreme Self, but this abiding knowledge that existence has no separateness can at one stroke remove all our mental agonies. This can be achieved only through sustained self-inquiry.

> *Utter darkness prevailed before the beginning with no*
> *existence of any kind. The primordial void created the*
> *universe from its benevolent thoughts.*
>
> Rig Veda

> *In the boundless ocean of consciousness, waves of*
> *phenomenal worlds appear and disappear. Eternal*
> *consciousness, which is the cause of all perceptions, is*
> *unaffected by the rise and fall of a universe at the end of*
> *its allotted time.*
>
> Ashtavakra Gita

*The cosmic vacuum was the original cause of creation of
the universe, life, and our thoughts. Our achievements are
only reflection of its infinite wisdom. Can any human
being subsisting in the endless ocean of consciousness claim
originality or individuality?*

MANDUKYA UPANISHAD

*There is no parallel to Him,
Whose glory is truly great.*

YAJUR VEDA

Loka Samasthath Sukhino Bhavantu!

Pavanaaya Namaha!
Salutations to the Purifier!

9

Desha and Kaala
Exploring Space and Time

*In religion, India is the only millionaire—the one land
which all men desire to see and having seen once by even
a glimpse, would not give that glimpse for all the shows of
all the rest of the globe combined.*

MARK TWAIN

*Lead me into that state of eternal light,
That light that shows the way to
Perpetual, undecaying, and immortal bliss,
May my heart turn toward the love
Of the resplendent Lord,
The source of all light,
Speed fast, then O mind!
And unite with the source of eternal bliss.*

RIG VEDA

Time is the most mysterious of God's powers. We really don't know how or why we calculate time. It has always been one of Nature's untameables. Even though the mind has created it, the mind cannot understand it. Time finds no place in Advaita Vedanta though space gets some prominence. Space is a positive entity. It is a product. Time, on the other hand, is a nonentity. It is not a product.

In reality, there is nothing like time. Advaita Vedanta says that it is purely a mental concept. In the absence of any activity or event, there cannot be any mental concept of time. With the occurrence of more than one event, the mind constructs the concept called "time." After the dissolution of the cosmos and before the next creation starts, Brahman alone remains. No events occur in that nonfunctional state. This is a timeless condition. Time exists as a concept due to the occurrences of many events taking place between creation and dissolution. The intellect conceives of these events as a series happening in time! When the universe does not exist, time does not exist. Even when it exists, it is not a real entity but merely a psychological concept!

Classical physics had always regarded space and time as independently existing realities. The so-called elementary building blocks of the universe, atoms, were presumed to be absolutely solid, impenetrable, indestructible, and unchangeable. So Einstein's theory of matter was a big shock to classical physics, not to mention his theory of relativity. Einstein and many of the scientists who came after him proved that time and space are relative. This is a shocking idea to us even now, bound as we are to our clocks and time schedules.

Time exists because things or events seem to happen. They move in relation to each other. What about space? It only exists if something binds it on either side. Distance is a measurement of the space existing between two objects. Einstein said that one cannot talk about space without bringing in time. If all objects ceased to exist, there would be no space and no time, since time cannot exist without space.

The fact that time and space are not eternal verities but convenient suppositions of the mind was well known to the rishis. They declared that human life is completely conditioned by the three *upadhis* (conditionings) known as *desha, kaala,* and *nimitta*—space, time, and causation. Everything we see in the world exists in space for a certain period of time and has a cause. This is how the mind works. Without these three upadhis, the mind cannot function.

THE IMPORTANCE OF MOTION

Einstein said that time and space are both relative to speed. As speed is derived by dividing distance (space) by time, both time and space depend on motion. The faster you go the more slowly time seems to move. The example of a pair of twins, who are twenty years old, is given. One twin travels in a spacecraft at 9/10 of the speed of light. He returns to the earth when he is forty-six years old, but finds that his twin has already turned eighty!

The same phenomenon is described in our Puranas, which shows that they were well aware of the fact that velocity reduces time. In the *Bhagavad Purana,* a king called Raivathan goes with his daughter, Revathi, to the world of Brahma and stays there only for the duration of a few minutes but when they return, the whole world has changed. None of the people the king had known existed any more. They were already dead and gone. Moreover, he finds that people have shrunk in size, whereas he and his daughter were very tall. He could not find anyone to marry his daughter, as no one could match her in size. At last he found that the only man who could match her was Balarama, Lord Krishna's brother. There are many other instances that demonstrate that the ancients were well aware that time, space, and velocity are irrevocably bound together.

Without change and movement, nothing can exist even for a moment. The stars are revolving, the planets are rotating, the galaxies are moving, and the whole universe is expanding. This is applicable to the subatomic world also where every particle is constantly in motion. This movement is what gives rise to the illusion of space and time! The

Sanskrit word for the world is *jagat*—that which is ever moving and ever changing. The choice of the name *jagat* for the world demonstrates that the ancients knew this important fact.

THE MEANING OF NOW

Pure energy as it exists on the quantum level is not bound by time or space but exists as a vast continuum of fluctuating change, which exists here and now. This moment, this tiny bit of time and space in which we now exist, is the only truth and reality. The past is a dream and the future a fantasy. What exists is the present, which has only a fleeting reality. Even as you read this, this present that you and I think is real has already slipped into an irretrievable past and the dreamt-of future has come and been swallowed up by the present.

What do we know about the exact meaning of the word *now*? If the past has already gone and future has not yet come, then all that exists is "now." So how long does "now" last? If the future already exists, then "now" is simply a moving finger agitating each preexisting moment as it passes. Does this mean that the future already exists in some nebulous form, which takes shape as we move toward it and as it gets focused upon by our consciousness? When we have something urgent to be done, ten minutes pass like one. If, however, we are waiting for someone to come, then ten minutes appear to drag on forever.

Time and space cannot be cut up into units smaller than the smallest unit, which is called *minima*. Parmenides, the Greek philosopher, came to the conclusion that Being consisted of only one thing or one unit. Of course this is what the ancient rishis have always emphasized: reality is one. It cannot be divided and cut up into bits. Since space-time is a combined unit made up by the mind, it also cannot be cut up into bits. However, this is what the mind tries to do all the time and thus it becomes frustrated. The human being is the only one in the animal kingdom able to conceptualize past, present, and future and thus the only being that is aware of the process of change, aging, decay, and death. This is why we are obsessed with death, mortality, and the end of time.

CYCLES OF ILLUSION

The great sage Vasishta is supposed to have told Rama:

> Countless have been the universes that have come into being and then dissolved. In fact even now countless universes exist at this moment and it would be impossible to conceive them in our minds. However they can be immediately realized in one's own heart, for these universes are the creations of the desires that arise in the heart, like castles built in the air. Human beings conjure up this world in their hearts and keep on strengthening the illusion of reality during their lifetime. When they pass away, they conjure up the worlds beyond and experience those. Thus there are worlds within worlds just as there are layers within layers in a banana stem. Neither the world of matter nor the modes of creation are truly real, yet the living and the dead think and feel that they are real. Ignorance of this truth helps to propagate and give a semblance of reality to this illusory creation!

The moment we demarcate ourselves as belonging to a specified place and time, that moment we separate ourselves from our roots, thus bringing suffering on ourselves. We are the creators of time and space. When we bring energy to conscious awareness, through the act of perception, we create separate objects that exist in space through a measured continuum called time.

As we have seen, Brahman alone is said to be sat or pure existence. Thus, Brahman is beyond time. The jagat or world is *mithya* (unreal or illusion); it has a dependent and relative existence. It is not eternal and timeless but exists on the substratum of Brahman. The universe has a beginning and thus it also has an end. Time starts with the beginning of the universe and ends with its dissolution. Space is born with the origin of the universe and expands and contracts, finally dissolving with the dissolution of the universe.

Western religion has always claimed that the universe is only six thousand years old but the rishis have always contended that our present cosmos is billions of years old, and that it is just one of many such universes that have arisen and dissolved in the vastness of eternity. The birth of our solar system has been poetically described in the Puranas as has already been mentioned. The Puranas talk about the milky ocean, which is of course the Milky Way. Through the will of the Creator, a vortex shaped like a lotus rises from the navel of eternity (Vishnu). It was called Hiranyagarbha, the shining womb. It gradually coalesced into our world, but it will perish some day billions of years hence, when the sun expands to many times its present size, swallowing all life on the earth. In the end, as the Puranas proclaim, the ashes of the earth will be blown into space by the cosmic wind. It is only with the birth of the twentieth century that we can understand this to be a beautiful simile for the fate of our planet!

CALCULATIONS OF TIME

Even though they denied any absolute existence to time, the rishis still had their own method of calculating time as it is an obvious fact of our human life. Sanskrit includes words for segments of time from microseconds to millennia. They knew of light years. The lifespan of Brahma, the Creator, is known as a *kalpa,* which is the longest period of time that we can think of—millions of light years. They also had words to describe the most minute period of time, less than the blink of an eyelid.

Our ancient people knew about sundials but found that they could predict time only on sunny days and certainly not at night. So they made the ingenious device known as a water clock, which did not depend on the sun. A small copper vessel with a small hole was floated in a big bowl of water. The water would slowly filter into the small vessel; when it reached half an hour or one hour, as the case may be, it would sink to the bottom. At that time a gong would be struck to denote the time and a bead would be shifted in an abacus. Anyone who wanted to know the time could come and count the beads on the abacus and have a good idea of the time. The Buddhist and Jain monks would use these water clocks to time their meditation.

In Delhi and Jaipur, huge instruments were installed in places called "Jantar Mantar." The instruments were positioned so carefully that they can be used to determine the correct time of day exactly to the minute by observing the shadows they cast. Both these places have huge sundials as well as other instruments to gauge the position of the stars in the zodiac. The kings who constructed them wanted to prove how accurate the Hindu almanacs and calendars were. One Vedic calendar goes back three thousand years and another six thousand years. The Western world could not believe or did not want to believe that the ancient rishis were such experts in astronomy that they could actually make such accurate calendars. They insisted that the Hindus must have stolen their calendar from the Greeks. Actually, the opposite is true and the Greek calendar uses many of the words of the ancient Vedic calendar.

As we have seen, in order to aid their calculations, the rishis said that every cycle of creation consists of four yugas or eons: Satya Yuga, Treta Yuga, Dwapara Yuga, and Kali Yuga. We are now in the Kali Yuga. By astronomical observations of planetary movements, the exact date of the beginning of the Kali Yuga has been verified as 3102 BCE in the month of February at 2 hours, 27 minutes, and 30 seconds. The Western astrologer Alice Bailey says:

> The calculations of the Brahmins are so exactly confirmed by our own astronomical tables that nothing but actual observation could have given so correspondent a result!

This means that the Kali Yuga began 5,143 years ago. The Mahabharata war began thirty-six years prior to the start of Kali Yuga. If we check this with the dates given by Western scholars for the Mahabharata war, we will see that their dates are quite absurd and unscientific.

Manusmriti and *Surya Siddhanta* state that one kalpa is a thousand yugas. Aryabhatta, the great Hindu astronomer of the sixth century, gives a slightly different account of the yugas, which is simpler and more scientific. He says that one kalpa is one thousand and eight yugas. One manvantara or the age of one Manu (the universal patriarch and producer of the human race) is given in the *Surya Siddhanta* as seventy-one yugas while Aryabhatta says it is seventy-two yugas. One yuga is said to be 4,320,000 years in the *Manusmriti* and Aryahhatta confirms this. Both the older systems divided the yuga into four smaller yugas but Aryabhatta took them to be of equal duration, naming them as quarter yugas, the duration of each being 1,080,000 years. From this we can see that Indian astronomers were able to calculate time from microminutes to millennia long before European astronomers came to the picture.

THE IMPORTANCE OF THE STARS

Vedic astrology has always been sidereal or based on stellar positions. It determines the positions of the signs of the zodiac relative to the observable fixed stars. By contrast, the old Western method employed a topical zodiac, which determines the signs of the zodiac relative to the equinoxes and solstices. The sidereal zodiac takes the point of precession into consideration, whereas the topical ignores it. The precession is the tilting of the earth on its axis, which changes at a rate of 50 seconds per year and completes a whole cycle of the zodiac in about 25,800 years. Thus, if we know at what point in the sidereal zodiac the equinox occurs, we can determine the astronomical era and date. This is how Vedic seers determined the age of different planets. They used the most universal of all clocks, the stars. While such precessional changes are not noticeable in an ordinary human lifetime, in cultures that endure over centuries and millennia, they become obvious. From this we can gauge that the Vedic culture has emerged from the hoary past of the universe.

A sidereal month is not measured from one full moon to another but rather according to the moon's return to the same place among the fixed stars. Hence, a sidereal month has twenty-seven days. A sidereal year is marked by the time the sun returns to the same position in the fixed stars. A sidereal day is four minutes shorter than a regular day so there are 366 of them in a normal year. This orientation to a specific point in the sky causes the calendar to gradually slip backward with the precession of the zodiac. In other words, the indication of the precession is built into the Hindu calendar by using sidereal time. According to sidereal time, the position of the equinoxes moves back a week or so every five hundred years, which is about seven degrees on the zodiac. This is why the Hindus celebrate the sun entering the sign of Capricorn on January 14, as this is an observable sidereal position, whereas the Western topical calendar uses December 21 as the date of the winter solstice, but this date is now actually in the sign of Sagittarius.

Our Vedic astronomers said that the earth's revolution around the sun starts from the fixed point known as *mesha sankranti rekha,* which is the Alpha Aries point. This is why our astronomical new year's day starts on *mesha sankranti,* which normally falls on April 14. In Sanskrit it is known as *mesha vishuvath.* As usual, Hinduism connects science with spirituality. The time of the change of the sign from *meena* to *mesha (mesha sankranti)* is known as *punya kaalam,* or an auspicious time, hence spiritual practices done on this day have extra power.

When the Vedic seers observed the stars, they saw a different orientation than we see today. The points of the solstices and equinoxes fell among different stars than they do now. This is because of the slow changes in Earth's orientation to the constellations according to the precession of the equinoxes. The Vedas present ancient astronomical positions, which can give us the dates at which they existed.

Thus, Hindu astronomy is a highly specialized system that requires precise astronomical observations and shows an ongoing knowledge of the exact placement of the planets and equinoxes relative to the fixed stars. Hence, the knowledge which the ancients had about time and space was indeed formidable.

> *If I am asked which nation has been advanced in the*
> *ancient world in respect of education and culture, then I*
> *would say it was—India.*
>
> MAX MULLER, GERMAN INDOLOGIST

> *Distribute thy wealth to those who deserve it,*
> *And seek the love of God,*
> *The most precious treasure of life.*
>
> SAMA VEDA

Loka Samasthath Sukhino Bhavantu!

ॐ

Achintyaaya Namaha!
Salutations to the One beyond Thought!

10

Vedic Astronomy, Astrology, and Mathematics

From the Speed of Light to Leaves on a Tree

I seem to have been only a boy playing on the sea shore diverting myself now and again by finding a smoother pebble or a prettier shell while the great ocean of truth lay before me.

ISAAC NEWTON

The evolutionary energy of the Supreme Self created the universe, life, and the mind. Its infinite intelligence has enchained us to the endless conundrum of cause and effect.

MUNDAKA UPANISHAD

In the solitary regions of green valleys,
And the confluence of the rivers,
The sages obtain divine intuition.

Rig Veda

Modern astrophysics and astronomy tell us that our galaxy called the Milky Way, or Akasa Ganga in Vedic terminology, contains approximately 100,000 million stars. Each star is like our sun, having its own planetary system. We know that the moon moves around the earth and the earth moves around the sun along with the moon. All planets in our solar system move around the sun. Each of the above bodies revolves on its own axis as well. Our sun, along with its family, takes one round of the galactic center in 225 million years. All galaxies including ours are moving apart at a terrific velocity of 20,000 miles per second. The total kinetic energy generated by the galaxies moving at this speed creates an amazing sound, which acts as an umbrella and balances the total energy consumption of the cosmos.

The great fourteenth-century scholar, Sayana, in his commentary on a passage in the *Rig Veda* says, "With deep respect, I bow to the sun, which travels 2,202 *yojanas* in half a *nimisha*." What exactly does this imply? A *yojana* is about nine miles. A *nimisha* is 16/75 of a second. How much does this give us? 2,202 yojanas × 9 miles × 75/8 nimishas = 185,794 miles per second. Thus, Sayana, a Vedic scholar who died in 1387 CE, calculated that sunlight travels at the rate of 186,000 miles per second, based on information he gleaned from a hymn in the *Rig Veda* written at a time that we cannot even imagine. The amazing fact is that this happens to be the speed of light as calculated by modern physicists in the last century! Western scholars might say that this is a coincidence. If so, the Vedic tradition is filled with such coincidences!

Some Western scholars have claimed that the Babylonians invented the zodiac of 360 degrees around 700 BCE, perhaps even earlier. Many claim that India received the knowledge of the zodiac from Babylonia or even later from Greece. However, in the *Rig Veda,* the oldest Vedic text, there are clear references to a chakra or wheel of 360 spokes placed in the sky. The number 360 and its related numbers like 12, 24, 36, 48, 60, 72, 108, 432, and 720 occur commonly in Vedic symbolism.

For example, many Hindus use a *mala* or rosary of *rudraksha* seeds or *tulasi* beads containing 108 beads in order to do their *japa* (mantra repetition). There is a scientific reason for using this particular number as there is in everything prescribed by Hinduism. The diameter of the sun is about 108 times the earth's diameter. The distance between the earth and sun is approximately 108 times the sun's diameter. The distance between the earth and the moon is 108 times the moon's diameter. Incredible as it may seem, the rishis were well aware of these facts and that is why they declared the number 108 to be sacred. Had they given scientific reasons for this in those ancient times, nobody would have been capable of believing them. It is only now with the progress of modern science that we of the modern age can recognize these facts and marvel at the unbelievable intelligence of those amazing beings.

There is another reason why the number of beads in the Hindu rosary has 108 beads instead of 100. This mala represents the ecliptic, the path of the earth and moon across the sky. Hindu astronomy divides the ecliptic into four equal sections called *paadas* or steps. These paadas contain 27 stars called *nakshatras*. When you multiply 27 with 4, you get 108, and these mark the steps that the earth and moon take through the heavens. Each of these steps is associated with a particular planet and deity with which you align yourself as you turn the beads.

The 109th bead is known as the *meru* or guru bead and it comes in the very middle of the mala. After repeating the mantra and turning the mala around in your hand until you reach the central or guru bead, you stop, turn the mala around, and continue reciting the mantra while moving the beads in the opposite direction. The meru bead represents the summer and winter solstices, when the sun appears to stop in its course and reverse its direction in a dramatic fashion. By using a mala in this way we are actually connecting ourselves with the cosmic cycles governing our universe! The rishis were well aware of the fact that the macrocosm (solar system) is mirrored in us (the microcosm). Actually it is said that there are 108 steps between our ordinary human awareness and the divine consciousness at the center of our being. Each time we chant a mantra, we are taking another step toward our own inner sun!

THE POWER OF PRATIBHA

The *Surya Siddhantha* is the oldest surviving astronomical text in Hinduism. It is dated to the fifth or sixth centuries by Western scholars, though of course the text itself claims to come from a much older tradition. It says that the earth is shaped like a ball and on the very opposite side from India is a great city where the sun is rising at the same time as it sets in India. It claims that a race of *siddhas* or spiritual adepts live in this city. Mexico lies exactly opposite to India on the globe. The ancient rishis were obviously well aware of the great astronomers of Central America many centuries before the so-called discovery of America by Columbus. Today, we know that the Mayans and Incas had a highly developed astronomy.

Vedic astronomers were also able to describe the different planets and stars and had names even for Uranus, which is only a relatively recent discovery in the West. They even predicted the length of time until Hailey's comet would reappear.

The star called Antares is said to be the fifteenth brightest in the solar system. However, Hindus call it *jyestha,* meaning "biggest" or "eldest." Astronomers only recently discovered that it is fifty times bigger than other stars! Indian astronomers had identified it seven thousand years ago!

Arundhati and Vasishta are the names of two stars found in the constellation known as the Big Bear. They were considered to be just one star by Western astronomers. Hindu astronomers had found that they were actually two stars revolving round each other. They named the two stars after the great sage Vasishta and his wife Arundhati, who were supposed to be an exemplary couple. On the first night of their wedding, south Indian couples are asked to go and take a look at these stars so that they can also have a perfect marriage.

Now the question arises regarding how these people found out so much about the planets without any instruments. The reason is simple: the rishis were in perfect control of their minds. Instruments are only the extensions of a human being's inherent powers—the power to see, to hear, or to accomplish things he or she wants done. For example, a telescope allows us to see distant objects like the planets; a microscope allows us to see tiny objects. Unless we have eyesight, neither of these instruments will work. When these powers are highly developed in oneself, then one has them at his or her command by the mere power of thought without the need for instruments. So if the rishis wanted to find out about the planets or about anything else, all they had to do was to concentrate on that object and they were able to find out everything they wanted. This, of course, is an infallible method; that is why their findings have never been refuted up to the present day, whereas in the West one person discovers something and another later refutes it.

These ancient scientists were not just intellectuals; they were practicing yogis who had sharpened their intuitive intellect to hitherto unknown heights. The very first lines of the *Surya Siddhanta* say: "In the Golden Age a great astronomer named Mayan desired to learn the secrets of the heavens, so he first performed rigorous tapas. Then the answers to his questions appeared in his mind in an intuitive flash." In his *Yoga Sutras,* Patanjali Maharishi, the foremost of the great psychologists of India and the world, states that through *samyama* (concentration, meditation, and unbroken mental absorption) on the sun, moon, and pole star, we can gain all knowledge of the planets and stars. The next *sutra* (couplet) he wrote clarifies this by saying, "Through keenly developed intuition, everything can be known."

Highly developed intuition is called *pratibha* in Sanskrit. It is available to those who have completely stilled their minds and are capable of focusing their attention on one object with laser-like intensity. Since their minds are totally under control, they are not limited to the fragments of knowledge supplied by the five senses. All knowledge then becomes accessible to them. The traditional Hindu view is that pure consciousness contains all knowledge—past, present, and future—and thus it is the very source of universal knowledge.

The rishis were also able to intercept electromagnetic waves and tune in to things happening in other places without using a radio or TV. They could also explore other planets in their astral bodies, without the need for rockets and spaceships. As has been said, the microcosm is only a reflection of the macrocosm and thus everything that takes place anywhere in the cosmos can be known by the human being. The sciences of parapsychology and telepathy are all very new to the modern mind, but these phenomena were well known to the rishis.

EARLY MATHEMATICS

The discovery of zero is one of the greatest contributions of India to the world. In one of the Vishnu temples inside the Gwalior Fort, the figure of "0" is seen for the first time. The deep calculations made by Indian astronomers would have been impossible without the use of zero. This is an abstract concept and Hindus were experts in abstractions. The concept of Brahman is purely an abstract one. Therefore, they were quick to realize the need for something that was absolutely nothing, on which the whole edifice of the universe as well as of mathematics could be constructed.

India was the first to start using the digits from 1 to 9. From India their use traveled to Arabia; then, when it went to the West, they called them Arabic numerals. However, they actually came from India, as the Arabs themselves admitted. Europe was still using the heavily structured Roman numerals, which made arithmetic very clumsy and difficult. When these Indian numerals came to Europe in the third century, the Roman Catholic Church denounced them as being the work of the devil; as a result, they did not come into vogue in Europe until a couple of centuries later. This is an example of the deep distrust and dislike the Church had toward anything new. This is why Western science lagged so far behind India in those days.

The method of graduated calculations was documented in the *Pancha Siddhantika* (five principles), in the fifth century, but the technique is said to have come from the Vedas. In fact, the first reference to astronomy is found in the *Rig Veda*.

The value of *pi* was also calculated by Budhayana (sixth century). He also explained the concept that is now known as the Pythagorean Theorem.

Quadratic equations were explained by Sridaracharya in the eleventh century.

The largest number used by the Greeks and Romans was 10 to the power of 6, whereas Indians used numbers as big as 10 to the power of 53, with specific names, as early as 5000 BCE. Even now the largest number used in mathematics is tera, 10 to the power of 12.

NAKSHATRAS: SEEING STARS

Since the rishis were so good in astronomy, it follows that they were also very good in astrology. Astrology or *jyotisha* is one of the oldest sciences and has its roots in the Vedas. Our great seers could see into the future and make many predictions. The earth is the recipient of impact from other planets. The planets under which we are born have given us all our characteristics, both physical and mental. Apart from this, every moment of our lives we are under the domination of some planet or other, even though we may not know it. This is what makes us display erratic patterns of behavior at certain times. Very often we are unable to account for the changes in our "moods" as we say.

Vedic calculations are based on the moon because the moon is the closest planet revolving around the earth and draws all planetary energies toward the earth's environment. This system is totally different from that adopted by Western astrology, which bases its calculations on the sun. The sun takes thirty days to move from one zodiac zone to another and thus can give only limited information. The moon moves faster and has greater impact on life. Hence, Vedic astrology is more precise and goes into greater detail.

It takes fourteen days for the new moon to reach its fullness. This phase is known as the bright phase (*shukla paksha*). It then takes another fourteen days to proceed to the new moon state, which is the waning phase known as the dark phase (*krishna paksha*). There is an overlap of a day as the new moon and full moon appear on the fourteenth day. This double counting is overcome by subtracting one day to get a total of twenty-seven days in a lunar month. The moon thus takes twenty-seven days to circle the 360 degrees of the zodiac.

Each of these twenty-seven points of the moon is represented by a star or *nakshatra,* beginning with Asvini and ending with Revathi. These provide the moon with a different constellation for every day of the lunar month. This is a more scientific system and easier to compute than the twelve signs of the zodiac of the Western astrological system, in which there is a change of sign for the moon every two-and-a-quarter days. While each of the twelve signs of the zodiac consists of a thirty degree section of the heavens, the nakshatras cover an area of thirteen degrees and twenty minutes.

Each month of the Vedic calendar is named after one of these lunar constellations or nakshatras in which the full moon occurs. If we examine the nakshatra chosen to rule the month we find that they mark the beginning of their sign. These nakshatras begin with the one that marks the vernal equinox. The nakshatra marking the full moon of the winter solstice is thus mentioned as the first month of the year (Asvini).

Everyone is born under a particular nakshatra or star. These stars have also been broadly delineated as possessing god-like, demonic, or human tendencies. Of course these are only broad characteristics and our natures also undergo changes with the changing of the planets during our lifetime and even during the day or week or month. Based on the moon's movement around the earth and the earth's movement around the sun, the astrologer can predict with amazing accuracy the experiences that will occur in the lives of people living on earth. Likewise each planetary movement causes definite changes in the earth's environment as well as in the lives of those who live on this planet. The astrologer can identify the dynamic movements of energies by observing the position of the planets at the time of birth in the zodiac.

Using the Vedic astrological system and the data available at the time of your birth, an astrologer can determine your birth star and ruling planetary periods. Such periods will bring specific experiences. The sum of these periods is 120 years, which is supposed to be the lifespan of a human being. The astrologer identifies all the energies inhaled by you with your first breath, which determines the qualities of your physical, mental, and astral systems and thus predicts the highlights of your life. He then casts your horoscope from which he or any other astrologer can predict with a fair degree of accuracy the broad facts about your birth, the number of siblings that you have, your parents' status, academic status, marriage, career, success, health, accidents, and death. Of course, the experience of the astrologer who reads the horoscope is also of great consequence.

The time of manifestation of a baby from the mother's womb will determine its inborn characteristics, based on how the planets are positioned in the zodiac at the time of birth. Great importance is given in astrology to identifying the very first inhalation to determine the effects of all subsequent inhalations. But it is very difficult to get the exact four seconds of the time of a baby's birth. So the astrologer has to work around the time given by the parents.

A horoscope can only give broad outlines of the things that will happen to a person. Even though the astrologer can predict the future of a person, he cannot say why it is so and certainly he cannot control it. Hinduism says that the time of birth as well as everything concerning a person is determined by his or her past karmas. In fact, we come into this world to work out the effects of our karmas. The universal intelligence is what is always in control. Similarly, we can predict the weather but we cannot control it. However, by knowing the type of weather to expect it is possible for us to take necessary precautions, such as an umbrella if it is going to rain or a sun hat if it is going to be sunny. This is the way in which astrological predictions can help us in our lives.

There is a form of Indian astrology in which our past, present, and future lives are recorded. It is called Nadi Shastra and was written on leaves by great saints called *siddhas*. The history of Nadi astrology can be traced back more than two thousand years. It is said that the siddhas were perfected beings who could appear in different forms at different places. Most of them were great lovers of God, especially in his form as Shiva. Lord Shiva, pleased with their devotion, granted them incredible powers. The siddhas wrote their predictions on palm leaves, called *"nadi* leaves." Known as Brighu Patrikas in north India and Agastya Nadis in south India, they predict, with an amazing degree of accuracy, the whole life history of any person who consults one of the people who deciphers them. People are astounded to see that everything about them was written on that particular leaf thousands of years ago.

It might seem miraculous that siddhas who lived hundreds of years ago could have known about our lives. However, these great sages obviously connected themselves with that unified field in which everything exists—past, present, and future. These leaves are not only found for Indian residents but also for foreigners and other nationals belonging to different religions and creeds. Still, not everyone has a nadi leaf predicting his life. Only those who were related to these saints in a *poorva janma* (previous life) will have a nadi leaf.

These leaves were written in Sanskrit. The king of Tanjore, Serfoji II, was a true patron of art and sciences. So he stored these palm leaves in his palace library, called the "Sarasvati Mahal." He also had them translated into the ancient Tamil script, called Vatellezuthu. It so happened that the British acquired possession of these leaves during their rule and later sold them to a few families through auctions. These families have carefully preserved the nadi leaves, awaiting their moment of rendezvous with the intended recipients. These can be found in Tamil Nadu near the temple of Vaideesvaran and a few other places.

This raises another interesting question: are we capable of controlling our future? When our mind connects to the universal mind, which we call *chitta* in Hinduism, we are actually capable of controlling our future. Modern science has offered us the explanation of how this can be so. The chitta or unified field provides a holographic blueprint of the world for all time, past, present, and future. As our scriptures tell us, everything in the future already exists in the realm of pure potential. When we look into the future or the past, we help to shape it and bring it into being by the simple act of observation, just as we do with a quantum entity in the present. Information transferred through subatomic waves does not exist in time or space but in the ever present. The past and present blur into one vast here and now and our brain picks up these signals and forms our own future. Our future exists in some nebulous state that we may begin to actualize in this very present. This field is the field of all possibilities and what actually happens, happens because we will it to happen, either consciously or subconsciously.

UNPARALLELED VARAHAMIHIR

In the history of Indian astrology, Varahamihir stands unparalleled. He was the son of a brahmin called Adityadas and lived in Avanti (Ujjain). Both father and son were ardent devotees of the sun, as their names, which are themselves names of the sun, imply. Varahamihir was born in 499 CE and passed away at the age of eighty-eight in 587 CE. He wrote many books, including the *Pancha Siddhantika*, which deals with five principles of ancient astronomy. Had it not been for him, the details of the five ancient systems would have been lost. The *Vivahapatal* and *Yogayatra* deal with the auspicious times for marriage and journeys, which their names imply as *vivaha* means marriage and *yatra* means journey. The *Bruhajjataka* deals with individual horoscopes and is still regarded as the most authoritative work on the subject.

The *Bruhat Samhita* is his last work, and the most celebrated. It has 106 chapters and 4,000 *shlokas;* it includes everything pertaining to planets, asterisms, and the signs of the zodiac. One portion deals with architecture, sculpture, geography, iconography, econometrics, auspicious signs in human beings and animals like horses, elephants, cows, dogs, goats, and so on. It also deals with omens, water divining, and methods of making swords, perfumes, and cosmetics. It has chapters dealing with the science of precious stones, with botany, and other topics. Varahamihir was the first to construct a simple ingenious water clock, as described in the previous chapter. He is the earliest authority on Vaastu Shastra, the science of architecture. He describes in great detail the many ways in which to build houses and temples and make sculptures. He gives the types and dimensions of dwellings for different members of society, from palaces for kings to officers, royal astrologers, preceptors, physicians, and laypeople. He details twenty types of temples and even suggests auspicious types of flowers and trees to be grown near dwellings and temples. His genius is brought out in these details.

He had a profound knowledge of astronomy. He was the first who declared the shape of the earth to be spherical. He wrote, "All things that are perceived by the senses are witness to the fact of the globular shape of the earth and refute the possibility of its having any other shape." The famous Arab Indologist Al-Beruni frequently referred to two Indian astronomer-astrologers—Varahamihir and Brahmagupta—as excellent astronomers who spoke only truth.

When acute water scarcity hit Gujarat in 1980, scholars went through the *Bruhat Samhita* and discovered a few simple methods given by Varahamihir to detect underground water.

1. If there is a termite hill in the east, near a Jambu tree, then sweet water will be found two head's deep to the right of the termite hill.

2. Sweet water that will not dry will be found three and a quarter head's deep and three arm lengths in the south from a Nagoda tree, shading an anthill.

Many such methods are given in the book, which has been found to be absolutely correct. He also gives details on the method of constructing tanks and ponds for storing water for long periods! His uncanny methods of locating groundwater veins could not possibly have been discovered in a human lifetime, solely by physical digging. It is much more likely that his revelations sprang from the insight he acquired through meditation and other *sadhanas* (or forms of spiritual practice).

ARYABHATTA, INDIA'S GREATEST ASTRONOMER

Aryabhatta was the greatest astronomer and mathematician of ancient India. He was described by the later astronomer Bhaskaracharya:

Aryabhatta is the master who, after reaching the furthest shores and plumbing the inmost depths of the sea of ultimate knowledge of mathematic, kinematics, and spherics, handed over the three to the learned world.

He developed theories that were "discovered" many centuries later by Western scientists. He was the first to gift algebra to the world. He cites his date of birth with astonishing accuracy in his famous work, *Aryabhatiya*: "When sixty times six years and three-quarters of a yuga had elapsed of the current yuga, I had passed twenty-three years since my birth." This means that in the year of Kali Yuga 3600, he was twenty-three years old. The Kali year 3600 corresponds to 499 CE. So he was born in the year 476 CE in Pataliputra, modern Patna in Bihar, where the famous university of Nalanda was located.

Aryabhatta was designated as the head of this university where a special observatory existed for studying astronomy. He was known as Ardubarius in Europe in the Middle Ages. Though he wrote two books, only the *Aryabhatiya* has survived. It deals with astronomy and mathematics and is the first Indian text to record the most advanced astronomy in the history of ancient science. Some of his findings:

- The value of *pi* = 3.1416; this is the same as we use today. Yet even this value he calls *aasaana* or approximate.
- Two methods of computing the sine table.
- The theory of solving indeterminate equations.
- The earth is spherical and it rotates. The period of one sidereal rotation of the earth in *Aryabhatiya* is given as 23 hours, 56 minutes and 45.1 seconds. The modern value is 23 hours 56 minutes and 45.091 seconds.
- He determined the length of the solar year from the heliacal risings of some bright stars at an interval of 365 and 366 days. According to him the year is 365 days, 6 hours, 11 minutes, 29.64 seconds! This value of the solar year is nearer to the modern value than that of Ptolemy. Based on his own observations, his astronomical constants differ from those of other astronomers and are more accurate than those of previous astronomers. The epicycles of the planets given by earlier astronomers, including Ptolemy, are fixed in value. Those given by Aryabhatta vary from place to place and yield better results.
- He gave the correct method for calculating the celestial latitude of both superior and inferior planets.
- His book is perhaps the earliest text on astronomy to use the radian measure of 3438 units for the radius of the circle.
- He was the first to describe the true cause of lunar and solar eclipses—that they were due to the shadow of the earth and moon. He also said that the moon was inherently without light but was illuminated by the sun.
- His theory of the earth's rotation and orbit round the sun was

expressed a thousand years before Copernicus put forward his heliocentric theory.

There is no doubt that Aryabhatta was a genius in both astronomy and mathematics. According to Georges Ifrah, at the beginning of the sixth century CE, Aryabhatta had perfect knowledge of zero and the place value system to calculate the square root and cube root, since these two operations could only be carried out by using the place-value system with nine distinct numbers and a tenth sign, which performed the function of zero.

BHASKARACHARYA

The period between Aryabhatta and Bhaskara is considered to be the golden age of astronomy in India. Bhaskara, son of Maheswara, was born in 1114 CE. It was his father who taught him mathematics. From the time of Aryabhatta, mathematics came to be incorporated into astronomy, which also required knowledge of geometry, trigonometry, arithmetic, and algebra. Bhaskara's son, Lakshmidhara, and grandson, Chanagadeva, also became renowned astronomer-mathematicians. However, Bhaskara's works are unparalleled. He was so thorough that he left no room for improvement.

Bhaskara's first work, which he wrote at the age of thirty-six, was *Siddhanta Shiromani;* it is divided into four sections called *Bijaganit, Grahaganit, Goladhyaya,* and *Lilavati,* this last book named after his daughter. He was the first to discover gravity, five hundred years before Newton. His last work at the age of sixty-nine was *Karanakutuhal.* This is used even today to make calendars. However, his *Lilavati* is the most acclaimed of his works. It is said that a person adept in the *Lilavati* can even compute the exact number of leaves on a tree!

The *Lilavati* deals with mathematics, addition, subtraction, division, squaring, cubing, extraction of square and cube roots. He gives names to all the main numbers in this work.

His *Bijaganit* is a systematic and complete treatise on Hindu algebra. His greatest contribution was the method of solving problems of indeterminate equations of the second degree. For these he gave both algebraic and geometrical solutions.

The *Grahaganit* and *Goladhyaya* deal with the astronomy of heavenly bodies based on the *Surya Siddhanta*. In the third chapter, he describes the situation of the earth, unsupported in space, and how beings exist on the surface of this spherical earth. He deals also with the circumference, surface area, and volume of the earth, using *pi* as 3.1416. He calculates the length of the sidereal year, the time taken for the earth to revolve round the sun, as 365.2588 days. The modern value is 365.2563, with a difference of only 3.5 minutes!

The fifth chapter looks at the mean motions of the sun, moon, and planets. The sixth and eighth chapters show how to calculate sunrise by calculating the lunar crescent, how to find out the relative lengths of days and nights in different seasons and latitudes. It also teaches how to find the latitude of a place.

The next three chapters deal with eclipses and another chapter deals with astronomical instruments used for observing heavenly bodies. At the end he concludes that intelligence is a better tool than all instruments!

There is an interesting story in connection with his daughter Lilavati. When he made his daughter's horoscope, he found a bad omen in it. If her marriage did not take place at a certain specified time, she would become a widow. At the time of her marriage, he made a water clock to know the exact time. He floated a small vessel with a hole at the bottom in a vessel filled with water, telling her that the small vessel would sink at the auspicious moment. He placed the device in a room and warned her not to touch it. However, curiosity prompted her to go near and look into it. A pearl from her nose-ring fell into the cup and caused it to sink. Hence, the marriage took place at an inauspicious time; as he had foreseen in the horoscope, Lilavati became a widow. Bhaskara realized that, however brilliant an astrologer may be, he can only predict the position of the stars. He cannot control them! They are controlled by the law of karma. However, to console his daughter and give her eternal fame, he named his masterpiece after her.

Bhaskara was the last of the great astronomer-mathematicians of ancient India. After his time, wave after wave of foreign hordes started invading and desecrating and destroying the land. Such a war-torn land was not the place for genius to flourish. But by this time Bhaskara's fame had spread to all parts of the then-known world including Arabia and Persia.

PLANETARY ENERGIES

When we look at the history of the world and the stories of our epics, and so on, we will see that aggressive forms of life seem to exceed optimistic and peaceful life-forms in number and intensity. This shows in our lives also. Negative and dominant thoughts seem to overwhelm optimistic feelings all too often. The reason for this can be found in the organization of the planets in our solar system. There are nine planets in the zodiac—the sun, moon, Mars, Mercury, Jupiter, Venus, Saturn, Rahu (Uranus), and Ketu (Neptune). Of these only Mercury, Jupiter, and Venus discharge positive energy. The moon can be positive or negative depending on its position in the zodiac. The remaining five planets discharge negative energy. This is why we find negative forces easily overcoming the positive in both our external life and inward life.

No matter how much modern science may deny the effect of planets on our lives and scorn the astrologer as old-fashioned and unscientific, these facts cannot be denied. The only way we can overcome these evil forces is to increase the positivity in our own lives and begin to show compassion for everyone and every creature. This is the lesson of the Vedas. Of course the highest method is what is given in the Upanishads—to align yourself to the highest force in the universe—Brahman; then the planets can never harm you. The planets all exist in the level of space and time and the one who has gone beyond and become one with the Absolute will be above all the effects of the planets!

It is to be hoped that modern science will eventually come to realize that the planets are indeed emitting invisible energies, both positive and negative, which pass through our bodies and give certain directions to our minds. If science accepted these facts then scientists would start to concentrate their minds on how to increase or decrease these energies in order to bring about a peaceful atmosphere both in the individual and the world. The ancients, however, discovered these facts and have given us certain methods for protecting ourselves. These will be dealt with in the next chapter.

> *The aforesaid constellations in the heavens, the mid-*
> *regions, observed in waters and on earth, on the*
> *mountains and in all quarters as the moon passes by*
> *them, revealing them, may they all be peaceful to me.*
>
> ATHARVA VEDA 8.9.2

> *The all-controlling, immortal wheel of the Universe*
> *Is revolving in infinite space,*
> *Ten, yoked together, draw it in this wide world.*
> *The wisdom of God, united with Cosmic Energy,*
> *Manages the whole Universe,*
> *On this Energy rest and depend*
> *All regions and planets.*
>
> ATHARVA VEDA

> *You grope in the darkness of ignorance seeking the elusive*
> *goal of your spiritual quest. But it lies deep in your own*
> *mind and becomes visible only to those who care to look*
> *inward.*
>
> YAJUR VEDA

Loka Samasthath Sukhino Bhavantu!

Sundaraaya Namaha!
Salutations to the Beautiful One!

11

Scientists of Hinduism
Revealers of the Secrets of Creation

*Indeed if I may be allowed the anachronism, the Hindus
were Spinozites more than 2,000 years before the existence
of Spinoza; and Darwinians many centuries before
Darwin; and evolutionists many centuries before the
doctrine of evolution had been accepted by the scientists of
our time and before any word like evolution existed in any
language of the world.*

SIR MONIER WILLIAMS

*Many of the advances in the sciences that we consider to have
been made in Europe were in fact made in India centuries ago.*

GRANT DUFF, BRITISH HISTORIAN OF INDIA

*Mayest thou, O Lord of vitality,
traversing through the misty Heavens,*

Listen to our prayers.
Mayest thou, O circumambient wind,
Listen to our invocations.
Mayest thou, O crystal clear water-laden cloud,
As thou floatest around the towering mountains,
Listen to our call.

RIG VEDA

Spirituality is the basis of Indian science. In India, not only science but art, music, and sculpture are all based on our spiritual roots and are thus aimed at taking us to the summum bonum of life, which is the attainment of unity with the Absolute. India has produced countless scientists through the ages whose discoveries, made with absolutely no modern instrumentation, astound the modern mind. While here we are only able to touch upon the lives of a few of these fascinating personages, they are representative of the intelligence and ability of the scientists of India, who fathomed the secrets of creation through their tapasya (austerities).

The Vedic rishis insisted that both para vidya (spiritual knowledge) and apara vidya (secular knowledge) were important. The later scientist-sages, who were responsible for giving us so much scientific knowledge, perfected their bodies, minds, and intellects to serve as fine-tuned laboratories. Their inner light and divine grace was what enabled them to achieve so much.

GREAT PHYSICIANS

O supreme Lord,
Let eminent scholars,
Possessing the luster of spiritual knowledge,
Be born in our country.

YAJUR VEDA

Western science even now cuts up Nature into different parts and probes into these various aspects as if they were totally unconnected. Western doctors also cut up the human being into parts and have specialists for the different parts—the nose, the eyes, the feet, and so on. They like to believe that both the human being and Nature are a conglomerate of different parts and have shut their eyes to the fact that both are actually wholes. It is better to treat the human being as an organic whole than as a collection of parts; the same applies to Nature.

Medical science in Hinduism is known as Ayurveda, which is the most holistic medical science in the world. It is the science of life and health, not of disease and death. Ayurveda or "the science of long life" forms a part of the *Atharva Veda*. It tells us how to remain healthy rather than telling us how to treat ourselves after we contract a disease. It makes use of Nature and natural substances to create health. The sun, air, water, and earth are all used for curing the body as well as many herbs provided by Nature. These sage-scientists were great botanists, with incredible knowledge of plants and herbs.

In fact, all the plants associated with the worship of the great gods of the Hindu pantheon are actually herbs. The *tulasi* plant, connected with Vishnu and his avataras, has great medicinal properties. A decoction made out of its leaves gives great relief if taken at the onset of a cold. The *bilva (vilva)* leaf that is essential in the worship of Shiva also has amazing curative properties. The fruits of this tree are a unique cure for all types of stomach problems. *Dhruva* grass, used in the worship of Ganesha, has great medicinal value. If the juice of this grass is kept in the mouth, it is of great help in curing gum problems. Everyone was encouraged to grow these plants so that common complaints could be cured by resorting to the herbs growing in their own gardens. The names of all these life-giving herbs have been detailed in the great books on Ayurveda.

Dietetics is a very new idea in the West but from ancient times it was said in Ayurvedic books, "Let food be your medicine and medicine your food." So they were well aware of the importance of a good, healthy diet in order to maintain their health. They knew that prana or the vital breath of the universe was what kept the body in health and not the use of externally injected medicines. Prana can only be revitalized by eating life-giving foods.

Dhanvantari

Born in 1000 BCE, Kashirau Divodas Dhanvantari, the king of Kashi, is hailed as the father of surgery in Ayurveda. Dhanvantari's teachings and surgical techniques were compiled by his foremost pupil, Sushrut, in the *Sushrut Samhita,* which has survived over the ages. Dhanvantari laid great emphasis on the study of anatomy using cadavers. He described how a dead body should be preserved so that it could be used by his students who were learning surgery. He made his students practice internal surgery with the use of many different things like gourds, watermelons, and so on in lieu of the foam materials that are used today. He also invented 20 sharp and 101 blunt instruments to be used in surgical operations. Some of his surgical procedures included skin grafting and the removal of stones from the bladder and urethra by perineal incisions. The German scholar Jurgen Thorwald was greatly impressed by the successful operations performed by Indian village surgeons exactly as described thousands of years ago in the *Sushrut Samhita* and said, "Nowhere in the world do we find such a conception."

Dhanvantari also made contributions in the fields of physiology and anatomy, as well as pharmacology (*dravya vijnana*), materia medica, and therapeutics (*chikitsa vijnana*). He gave a complete theory of drug composition, the molecular structure, psycho-chemical properties, and the therapeutical action of food and drugs. He based these on the ancient Nyaya system (one of the six systems of Indian philosophy), of *paramanus* (molecules) and *anus* (atoms). Some of his findings have led modern scholars to call him a molecular biologist.

He was the first to cite the hemopoietic or blood-forming factor in the *yakrut* (liver) and the role of both liver and spleen in the formation of blood. He prescribed goat liver for anemia and night blindness. Many such original discoveries can be listed, which originate in ancient India, coming from Dhanvantari and his disciples.

Sushrut

Sushrut compiled the teachings of his guru Dhanvantari in the *Sushrut Samhita*. During his era surgery formed a major role in general medical practice. It was known as *shalya-tantra*. Sushrut details many surgical procedures in obstetrics, orthopedics, and ophthalmology. He describes a method of removing cataracts known today as "couching." This method was successfully practiced by Indian surgeons till the first half of the twentieth century. Sushrut introduced the concept of anesthesia, using intoxicants such as wine and cannabis. He was the first to do plastic surgery. His method of repairing a broken nose is known as rhinoplasty and was in vogue till the beginning of the twentieth century. The concept of plastic surgery came to the West only after the First World War.

The details he gives of human embryology are mind-boggling. These observations are possible today only with the aid of microscopy, X-rays, and ultrasound. He mentions that the fetus develops seven layers of skin, naming each layer and the specific diseases that may affect that layer in adulthood. He was aware of diseases due to genetics and mentions congenital defects acquired from parents.

Besides trauma involving general surgery, he gives an account of the treatment of twelve varieties of fractures and six types of dislocations, which would confound orthopedic surgeons today. He meticulously detailed both pre- and postoperative procedures. He even showed methods of treating scars after the wound had healed. No single surgeon in the history of science has to his credit such masterly contributions in terms of basic classification, thoroughness of the management of disease, and a perfect understanding of the ideal to be achieved.

His excellence in surgery and original insight in all branches of medicine render him the most versatile genius in the history of medical science. The examples cited here remind us that these great souls of Ayurveda practiced an astonishingly scientific, sophisticated, and advanced art of medicine as early as the third and second millennium BCE. Several millennia later, so-called modern medicine is retreading these beaten paths! Sushrut attributed his inventions to the excellence of his guru Dhanvantari and divine grace invoked by his personal sadhana.

Charak

Charak has been cited as India's most outstanding medical practitioner. *Char* means to move about. Therefore, it appears that Charak was a wandering teacher who practiced and propagated his knowledge by constantly traveling from village to village to relieve human suffering.

Four thousand years ago, the rishi Agnivesh compiled an Ayurvedic treatise called the *Agnivesha Samhita*. Around 800 BCE, Charak redid this *Samhita,* which became renowned as the *Charak Samhita*. Its fame spread beyond the borders of Bharatavarsha (ancient India). By 987 CE, it had been translated into Persian and then to Arabic. Al-Beruni, the noted Arabic physician, confessed that his chief source of medicines was this Arabic edition. The famous Arab physician Serapion often referred to Charak as "Sharak Indianus" in his medical treatise.

The *Charak Samhita* consists of 120 chapters in eight sections. His work has deeply impressed many modern physicians. Dr. George Clarke of Philadelphia observes:

> If modern physicians would stop the use of modern drugs and chemicals and treat their patients according to the methods of Charak, there will be less work for the undertakers and fewer chronic invalids in the world!

The human body is composed of the *pancha mahabhutas* or the primary five elements—earth, water, light, air, and space. The body's constitution is based on the three *doshas* or humors known as *vata, pitta,* and *kapha,* which refer to the quantity and quality of air, bile, and phlegm present in the system. When their equilibrium is disturbed, disease sets in. Two thousand years before Harvey, the concept of blood circulation was well known in Ayurveda. Charak described the heart as the controlling organ of blood circulation. He said that the body is composed of *dhamanis*—large and small vessels—which supply nutrition to the tissues and remove waste products from them.

He refuted the theory that germs were the only cause for disease. Different types of germs may flourish in the body only if favorable conditions prevail. He attached great importance to the digestive fire or *jadaragni* within us to maintain vitality, energy, and *ojas* (physical splendor). He clearly described the digestive process and its end products, which are remarkably similar to those discovered by Western science. He said that when the digestive fire was either increased or decreased, disorders would result.

His treatment consisted of a system of *mahakashayas,* each concoction including ten herbal preparations, for various diseases. The Pancha Karma treatment, which has become so popular now, was given to rejuvenate and cleanse the body. Charak treated the patient as a whole rather than just a specific disease. In addition to medications, he stressed the importance of diet, daily activity, and seasonal activity in the long-term health of an individual. He laid emphasis on prevention rather than cure. This was Ayurveda's unique approach to the understanding and treatment of diseases, which Charak followed faithfully.

He discussed the nature of epidemics, which can totally destroy a locality. He listed four contributing factors such as polluted air, water, place, and time. He also said that the root cause of epidemics was humankind's unrighteous behavior (*adharmic* acts). He was well aware of water-borne diseases and advocated drinking only boiled water during the rainy season.

He gives a fascinating account of visible *krimis* or parasites and microscopic *krimis* in the blood. In the absence of microscopes, his account of microbes will confound modern microbiologists. He said,

"These (microbes) are very minute and can be observed with a *yantra* (instrument)." We are left to wonder if he foresaw the discovery of the microscope! He was the first to identify and name such microbes. He even typified their symptoms: itching, needle-like piercing, pain, and an electric current-like effect. Such accuracy without a microscope is only possible for a *brahmanishta rishi* or one in a state of cosmic consciousness. This would enable him to observe the minutest functions of the body right down to the cellular level.

Inoculation against smallpox only began to be practiced in the nineteenth century in Europe but this was already in vogue during Charak's time. This was done by making four scratches on the forearm of the person with a special instrument and introducing the pus from a smallpox spore into the scratches. This was then bandaged and left for a few days. Every morning and evening, four pots of cold water were poured on the person's head to keep the fever in check. This treatment was most successful; during smallpox epidemics, in which normally forty out of one hundred died, the number was reduced to two out of one hundred.

Charak also showed how to plan, construct, and equip hospitals, including mental and obstetric hospitals. He gave minute details on accommodation, bathrooms, toilets, disinfection, medicines, equipment, and security. He even considered kitchens, which had to be warmed in winter. His hospitals included a section where healthy people could undergo rejuvenation therapy such as Pancha Karma thrice a year.

Charak laid great emphasis on the physician's integrity and control of the senses, including observance of *brahmacharya* (celibacy). According to him, medical practice was not for the fulfillment of any desire or gain but solely for the sake of removing suffering from humanity.

A physician who fails to enter the inner body of the patient with the lamp of knowledge and understanding can never treat him. Above all the doctor should be compassionate.

His excellence can be attributed mainly to his personal sadhana (spiritual discipline) which no doubt endowed him with many siddhis (miraculous powers). This gave him the phenomenal ability to document the medicinal qualities of thousands of plants and minerals during his lifetime without experimentation. It is said that, due to his sadhana, he was able to converse with plants as he walked through the forests. The plants would let him know their medicinal properties, which he would tell his pupils who were following behind him, who in turn noted them down.

Vedic Medical References

Here is a sampling of medical references in the *Atharva Veda*.

God pierced the seven openings in the head. He made these ears, these nostrils, eyes, and mouth through whose surpassing might in various forms bipeds and quadrupeds can complete their journey of life (10.2.6).

Just as light hangs between earth and firmament, so does Munja (a healing medicinal herb) cure fever and dysentery (1.2.4).

O patient suffering from urinary disease, just as the water of the flooded ocean rises and flows into streams so have I unclosed the orifice of thy bladder so that your urine can come out unchecked (1.3.8).

These veins serviceable like maidens, which run their course clothed in blood, must now stand quiet like sisters who are brotherless and bereft of power (1.17.1).

O patient we control your jaundice with the seeds of Shuka trees and other strong healing medicines (1.22.4).

O woman from thee we banish and expel the cause of sterility.
We lay this apart and far removed to another place (3.23.1).

The herb named Rohini is the healer of broken bones. Arundhati
is the wound healing herb. Heal thou this wound (4.12.1).

If some flesh consuming germ, entering my raw, cooked, half
cooked, or thoroughly cooked food hath injured me, let the
germs with their wives and offspring be destroyed so that I may
be free from disease (5.29.6).

THE PSYCHOLOGY OF PATANJALI

There are actually three rishis known as Patanjali but here we are concerned only with the great *yogacharya* (master of yoga), who wrote the
Yoga Sutras, commonly known as *Patanjali Yoga Darshana.* He is the
greatest and most ancient psychologist in the world. Even today there
is none greater than him. His works have been famous from ancient
times. Yoga was expounded in the *Rig Veda,* Upanishads, and Puranas.
However, it was Maharishi Patanjali who gave it a concise form in his
Yoga Sutras.

The word *yoga* comes from the Sanskrit word *yuj,* "to unite or join
or merge." The union of the jivatma with the Paramatma is known as
samyoga. The word *yoga,* as commonly bandied about in the modern
world, does not have the right connotation. It is actually what is known
as Hatha Yoga in India and is concerned with the perfection of physical health and purity with the aid of eighty-four *asanas* (postures) and
pranayama (control of prana through breath).

The yoga of Patanjali is also known as Raja Yoga; it focuses on
controlling the mind by the will. The aim is to eliminate all sources
of disturbances in the mind, whether external or internal, thus
making the mind responsive to the spiritual reality within. This is
a very different approach from that of modern psychologists, who

think of the ego and the libido as the basis of all mental disturbances.

Patanjali's yoga is also known as *ashtanga* (eight-limbed) yoga since he divides the process into eight parts or limbs. The first five are the external limbs of ashtanga yoga. The next three are the internal limbs.

1. *Yama:* These are the disciplines that apply to everyone and are five in number.
   a. *ahimsa* (nonviolence in deed, word, and thought)
   b. *satya* (truth)
   c. *asteya* (refraining from taking what belongs to others)
   d. *brahmacharya* (celibacy)
   e. *aparigraha* (detachment)
2. *Niyama:* These are the disciplines that one places on oneself.
   a. *shoucha* (purity)
   b. *santosha* (contentment)
   c. *tapas* (austerity)
   d. *svadhyaya* (study of the scriptures)
   e. *isvara pranidhana* (total surrender to God)
3. *Asana* (postures). The main reason for practicing asanas is to be able to master a posture so that one can comfortably stay in it for three hours without discomfort and be able to practice meditation without disturbance to the body.
4. *Pranayama* (control of the prana through breath). Prana is the vital air or life force. Regulation of prana induces steadiness of the body and mind and promotes peace. Pranayama also purifies the subtle nerve channels known as nadis. This is done by a method of controlling the breath. Many different types of breath control are given but they should be practiced with caution. While practicing, it must be kept in mind that the object of pranayama is the control of prana and not the mere control of breath. However, there is a close connection between prana and breath, which enables one to manipulate pranic currents by manipulating breathing.

5. *Pratyahara* (withdrawal of the senses). This is the control of the five senses by the mind and diverting them inward away from their respective objects.

6. *Dharana* (contemplation and concentration). The mind is made to fix itself on the object of contemplation until its movements cease. It becomes one with the essential nature of the object and can move no further. It has to be brought back again and again whenever it strays from the path.

7. *Dhyana* (meditation). This is an extension of dharana. Here there is an uninterrupted flow of the mind toward the object of meditation. The practitioner masters this stage only if she or he succeeds in completely eliminating all distractions.

8. *Samadhi* (superconscious state). This is an advanced state of dhyana in which the mind totally submerges itself in the object of meditation and nothing else remains. In other words the mind and the object become one.

Patanjali Yoga is often combined with other systems of liberation. Even the Buddhists took it up.

Evolution East and West

Patanjali explores all the facets of the mind and how to keep it on the evolutionary path, which is open to all human beings. Instead of degrading the human being into his animal origins, he uplifts him to his spiritual status. This understanding of evolution is very different from the biological findings of Darwin. In his theory of natural selection Darwin asserted that might is right and only the fittest would survive. This meant that the genetic terrorist who killed indiscriminately to save his own skin was the highest on the evolutionary ladder. The height of the evolutionary cycle was the superman who could conquer those who were weaker. Perhaps it was these views of life that led to terrorists like Hitler and Mussolini dominating the world through brute force, and many today who hold the world at ransom at the point of a gun.

However, there was an obvious flaw in Darwin's theory. Preservation of the species actually depends on the infant of every creature, but we find that the infant of every species is very weak and unable to look after itself. It can exist and grow only due to the love of the mother. Without this overwhelming love, from one who is prepared to sacrifice her own life to save her young, there would be no hope for any creature. So survival does not depend on being the strongest but on a most abstract and divine emotion called love. It is love that has ensured survival so far and in love lies our only hope of survival in the future.

The theory of evolution was well known to Patanjali long before Darwin came into the picture. The manifestation of latent powers is the reason why species evolve. This idea has been well expressed in a few words by Patanjali in the second aphorism of the fourth chapter of his *Yoga Sutras*. Vivekananda comments on this in his book on Raja Yoga: "The Evolution into another species is caused by the in-filling of Nature."

Kapila, the father of Hindu evolutionists, was the first to explain this theory through logic and science. Nature is filled not from outside but from within. Nothing is added to the individual soul from outside. The seeds are already there, but their development depends upon their coming in contact with the necessary conditions requisite for proper manifestation. There are instances of murderers and robbers suddenly becoming saint-like. Vedanta says that the moral and spiritual powers that remained latent in them have been aroused, and the result is a sudden transformation. No one can tell when or how the slumbering powers will wake up and begin to manifest. The individual soul possesses infinite possibilities. Each soul is studying, as it were, the book of its own nature by turning one page after another. When it has gone through all the pages, or, in other words, all the stages of evolution, perfect knowledge is acquired, and its course is finished.

When we read a book and we feel interested in a particular page or chapter, we will read it over and over again and will not open a new page or chapter until we are perfectly satisfied. Similarly, while going through the book of life, if the individual soul likes any particular stage, it will stay there until perfectly satisfied with it; after that it will go forward and study the other pages. One may read very slowly, and another very fast; but whether we read slowly or rapidly, each one of us is bound to read the whole book of our life and attain to perfection sooner or later. This is the great and beautifully reassuring teaching of Hindu psychology. No one is cast beyond the pale or damned for eternity.

The father of Western psychology, Freud had only read the pages of the book of life referring to our lower nature, which passes through each stage of animal life from the most minute bioplasm up to the present stage of existence. Patanjali, the father of Indian psychology, showed us the pages that deal with moral and spiritual laws, thus encouraging us to go forward to find our highest potential within our own psyche.

PANINI THE GRAMMARIAN

Sanskrit has a very intricate type of grammar. Of course many books have been written on Sanskrit grammar but Panini's (520–480 BCE) work is outstanding. He was developmentally delayed as a child and was expelled from the Gurukula (school where students resided along with their tutor and learned the Vedas). His guru showed him that the line of intelligence was missing from his palm. Panini was so incensed with this that he took a knife and carved the line on his palm.

He then went to the Himalayas and performed intense tapasya. Shiva was pleased with him and taught him the knowledge of Sanskrit grammar. Shiva rattled his *damaru* (small hand drum) fourteen times. Each sound became a Sanskrit *sutra*. Panini created a new method of Sanskrit grammar from these sutras. He listed about 1,700 basic elements of grammar and 4,000 rules of pronunciation, which made Sanskrit a most precise and scientific language, unequalled in the world. Everyone soon came to follow Panini's grammar. His famous work is known as the *Ashtadhyayi,* composed of eight chapters. In 1959, when John Backus, the inventor of the world's first computer language, was studying the grammar of many of the world's languages, he discovered that the rules described in the *Ashtadhyayi* were as mathematical and precise as his computer language.

Panini divided Vedic literature into two parts: Dhrusta, which includes the four Vedas, and Procta, which includes the Braahmanas, Kalpas, and Sutras. His work on Sanskrit grammar has remained unsurpassed to this day.

OTHER SCIENCES

Ancient India was also far advanced in metallurgy. The esoteric knowledge of how to stop iron from rusting is something that modern science has yet to discover. The huge iron pillar in Delhi was made a thousand years ago and is still shining as if it had been made the previous day. A similar rust-proof pillar can be seen in Bangalore; it was made by tribal peoples of the area to welcome Sri Adi Shankaracharya more than two thousand years ago.

For many thousands of years, India was the only country that knew the very difficult process of extracting zinc from ore. The Chinese came and learned this technique and the British took it from the Chinese. It was only in 1543 that the scientist called William Chapier made the first zinc extraction plant in England. Until that time, the only zinc available came from India.

The ancient art of making exquisite figures out of copper and bronze is still to be found in the city of Tanjore in Tamil Nadu. This was an ancient method in which wax was used to make a mold into which hot metal was poured, then encased in mud and heated. When the mud covering was broken, the wax would have already melted and the beautiful figure would stand revealed. We find a wealth of beautiful figures of the gods in Tanjore.

Ancient India was also famous for its wonderful temple architecture. The science was known as Vaastu; it is a unique form of construction since it takes into consideration the cosmogony of the universe. Everything is connected to the different directions. Generally, temples are strategically located in places where the earth's positive energy is abundantly available from the magnetic wave distribution of the north/south pole thrust.

All aspects of temple architecture and ritual have a scientific basis. The main idol is placed in the center, known as Garbhagriha or Moolasthan, over a copperplate inscribed with some yantra (spiritual design), very often the Sri Yantra (for details regarding the Sri Yantra, see chapter 12). The copper absorbs the earth's magnetic waves and radiates them to the surroundings. Thus a person who regularly visits a temple and makes a clockwise *pradakshina* (circumambulation) of the sanctorum receives the magnetic waves that are being beamed all over the temple. They are slowly absorbed by his or her body. This is a very slow process but Hinduism encourages daily visits to a temple; this allows the body to absorb more energy. The sanctum sanctorum is completely enclosed on three sides so the effect of all the energies is very high inside. The lamps radiate the heat and light energy.

The ringing of bells and the chanting of mantras produce sound energy in temples. The fragrance from the flowers and the burning of camphor radiate chemical energy. The effect of all these energies is activated by the positive energy that comes out of the idol.

During the time of the great Tamil king, Raja Raja Chola, many extraordinary temples were made in Tanjore, which was his capital, and places abroad. The Cambodian king invited him to send his artisans and architects; the famous temples of Angkor Wat in Cambodia were all built by Hindu craftsmen. The temple to Buddha called Borobodur in Java was also built by Hindu artisans. These temples are not only unique in their architecture but were also made in such a way that the main temple was on the same line of longitude as the main temple in Tanjore. Moreover, the temple door to the sanctum was constructed in such a way that the sun's rays fell straight to the foot of the deity during one or other of the equinoxes.

The same phenomenon can be perceived in the Buddhist cave carvings at Ajanta and Ellora. These caves are about seventy feet above the ground level and were all carved with the most incredible sculptures of gods and demigods from the inside of the cave where there is hardly any light. The caves seem to be in horseshoe formation and each cave was oriented toward some specific direction in order to be able to see a certain star or planet. The figure of the Buddha in the main stupa was so designed that the sun's rays would fall on him during the summer solstice. These types of designs show the astonishing knowledge the ancients had about cosmogony and cosmology. These caves are dated at 200 BCE.

Till the eighteenth century, India was the world leader in the making of cottons. The dyes that were used were purely natural and had brilliant colors. However, the British learned the techniques and started making their own cottons. India lost heavily because of this, since the British used machines while the Indians were still using handlooms. Silks were also produced in India from ancient times. The equal of the exquisite silk cloth from Banaras and Kanchipuram is still not found anywhere else in the world.

The English word *navigation* is derived from the Sanskrit word *navagatih,* or ship. The word *navy* also comes from the Sanskrit word *nav* (boat). The art of navigation was first started in the river Sindhu. When Vasco da Gama came along the shores of Africa in his search for India, he found some Indian merchants were already there before him with ships three times the size of his own. He was frightened to cross the ocean without keeping some land in sight, so the Indian merchants escorted his ship across the ocean. Europeans still thought the world was flat and were frightened of falling off the edge! But Vasco da Gama reached modern Goa with the help of the Indian sailors. Despite this, the West still believes the Portuguese were the greatest of all shipbuilders and navigators.

Ancient Hindus were also noted for the different types of games they played. Chess is known as Shatranj or Ashta Pada in Sanskrit; it was a game normally played by kings. Snakes and ladders and cards were also common.

The world's first university was in Takshashila, modern Afghanistan, which was a part of India in 700 BCE. Records show that over ten thousand students from all over the world came to study there and more than sixty subjects were offered. The University of Nalanda in Pataliputra (modern Patna in Bihar) was constructed in the fourth century and was one of the greatest achievements of ancient India in the field of education. The construction of this university is credited to Chanakya, who is famous for his treatise on political science known as *Arthashastra*. Of course, the official language of the university was Sanskrit.

> *Omniscient, you are unknown,*
> *Origin of all, you are self-existent,*
> *Lord of all, you are without a master,*
> *Though one, you divide into all forms.*

RAGHUVAMSA, KALIDASA

> *The Lord's joy manifests through the splendorous beauty*
> *and serenity of his creations.*
> *The supreme bliss of this divine love is felt within the*
> *soul that is pure and receptive to the sanctity of God's*
> *boundless love. It kindles the innermost self of devotees.*

SAMA VEDA 5.4.7

Loka Samasthath Sukhino Bhavantu!

Sarva-darshitaaya Namaha!
Salutations to the All-Seeing One!

12

Mantras and Yantras
The Power of Sounds and Symbols

Truth is within us, it takes no rise,
From outward things, whatever you may believe,
There is an inmost center in us all.
Where truth abides in fullness, and around,
Wall upon wall, the gross flesh hems it in,
This perfect, clear perception—which is Truth.

ROBERT BROWNING, *PARACELSUS*

SOUND ENERGY

The rishis were experts in the science of sounds known as phonetics. Sound is the softest but the most powerful form of energy in the universe. Mantras are sounds with a great scientific basis. The letters of the mantras constitute an alphabet of forms brought together in a capsule of form, sound, and power. They denote that formless Absolute that is beyond all forms yet is the cause of all forms. In fact we say that our world is the outcome of sound giving rise to forms.

We all know that most whirling objects produce a lot of sound. The planets whirling on their own axes, solar systems whirling around galaxies, and galaxies moving at 20,000 miles per second create an amazing sound. The sound thus generated cannot be heard by the normal human ear but it was heard by the rishis. They said that this was the sound of *Aum*, the cosmic hum of the Creator, the original sound that led to the formation of the universe. This discovery is attributed to the great sage Vishvamitra.

Gayatri Mantra

Vishvamitra is also the seer of the great mantra known as the Gayatri. This mantra has amazing propensities for taking us to higher levels of consciousness. Its greatness is only just being recognized by the Western world. The Gayatri Mantra is chanted thus:

> *Aum bhur, bhuvah, suvaha,*
> *Tat savitur varenyam,*
> *Bhargo devasya dhimahi,*
> *Dhiyo yona prachodayat.*

The first three words of the mantra are *bhur, bhuvah,* and *suvaha,* which stand for the three spheres: *bhur* stands for the earth sphere; *bhuvah* points to our galaxy with the sun at the center; *suvaha* stands for the super galaxies beyond ours. The Gayatri Mantra includes the totality of the energy generated in the universe and beyond in its sphere of influence. Thus, it has great force if used with faith and correct pronunciation. From this we realize how much the rishis knew about phonetics and cosmology!

The sound produced by the earth, planets, and galaxies is *Aum* (the name of formless God). That God (*tat*), who manifests in the form of the light of the sun (*savitur*) is worthy of respect (*varenyam*). We should, therefore, meditate (*dhimahi*) upon the light (*bhargo*) of that deity (*devasya*) and also chant *Aum*. May he (*yo*) guide our intellect (*dhiyo*) in the right direction (*prachodayat*).

Divinity of Sound

Aum is also known as the *pranava*, the primeval sound, which is the most important symbol in Hinduism to denote the Supreme. In fact it is the Supreme in the form of sound. It is the first of the cosmic sounds out of which everything else came. The chanting of every mantra should be preceded by *Aum*. The Vedas also start with this sound. It is the most well known and important mantra for meditation. Later on, other religions realized the importance of *Aum,* articulating it as *amen* and *ameen*.

The various gods of Hinduism are the outcome of this great science of sounds giving rise to forms. A mantra is actually a particular vibration of the original throb of the cosmos and represents the sound body of one particular god in the structure of consciousness. When the mantra of a specific god is used continuously, it will draw the power of that particular god to oneself. Mantras are chanted during rituals in order to invoke the appropriate deity. Many mantras are given in Hinduism to balance the positive and negative tendencies of the planets and promote a steadying effect on human life. According to this ancient science, when the mind chants these powerful sounds or mantras in order to achieve some definite purpose, certain specific changes will start to occur.

SYMBOLS FOR THE FORMLESS

Symbolism plays a great role in Hinduism, which makes use of mathematical symbols called *yantras* and *chakras* to denote the Supreme and to bestow auspiciousness on the user. While mantra is the sound form of the deity, yantra is the form pattern. In order to bring that formless and eternal Being into the vision of the ordinary human being, the rishis used their genius to express the formless Supreme as mathematical symbols. This made it easier for the common people to imagine the Infinite. We can understand this in light of the recognition that it would be impossible even for the greatest mathematician to work without the help of numerals for arithmetic. Algebra has to use numerous signs that are incomprehensible to the common person. The problem gets more complex as the numbers become larger and larger. If it is so difficult to do mathematics with finite numbers, imagine how difficult it would be to comprehend the Infinite without the help of symbols!

Machines and Instruments

The word *yantra* is derived from the root *yam,* "to control," and has been freely used in ancient India for any contrivance. The word actually means "a machine or an instrument." Ancient India produced many accessories known as *pakayantras* for scientific activities, such as surgical instruments and laboratory equipment in medicine. Many yantras used in astronomy are described in astrological works.

In the *Mahabharata,* we hear of the *matsya yantra,* which is a revolving wheel with a fish on top, which Arjuna had to shoot in order to win Draupadi in the *svayamvara* (marriage by choice of the bride). In the *Ramayana* Valmiki makes interesting references to yantras on the field of battle. He also claims that the fortifications of Ayodhya included equipment in the form of yantras. At one point Rama asks his brother, Bharata, whether a fort was equipped with yantras. Lanka, as a city built by the great architect Mayan, was naturally full of yantras. The city even had a special chamber filled with yantras.

We can see the continuity of this tradition in the later *Arthashastra* (political science) of Kautilya. This work from 300 BCE, a treatise on statecraft, speaks of yantras in connection with battles, as well as with architecture to some extent.

Household Sacred Geometry

If we look carefully at many flowers we will see incredible mathematical figures, forming what is known as the golden ratio. In fact it is found all around us—in flowers, in seashells, and the forms taken by desert sand when the wind blows through it. If one goes to a typical south Indian house one can see many strange drawings on the ground in front of the entrance. These are known as *kolams* in south India; the *rangoli* designs seen in north India are similar. They have existed in India from immemorial times and have obviously been drawn from the depths of the human psyche. They are symbolic representations of unseen forces. We don't know their origins. All we know is that they are considered to be auspicious and most traditional homes have them. Now of course since so many people dwell in apartments they are used only for auspicious occasions. They are part of the sacred geometry of the Hindus.

Modern technology has actually proved the natural existence of such designs, made by the vibrations of sound, the original source of all creation. With the help of something called a tonoscope, sounds made by the human voice can be viewed as turning into incredible shapes, the form changing with changes in pitch. The shapes are strikingly similar to kolams and rangolis. This again proves what our ancient rishis have always reiterated—that all the forms we perceive here have their source in a subtle field, which the physical eyes are unable to see. Hence their prayer, *asato ma sat gamaya*—"Lead me from the unreal to the real."

Spiritual Instruments

The yantras used for spiritual practices are a little different. The formless radiance emanating from the Infinite emits rays of definite forms and weaves them into the features of the various gods. The perfect lines of beauty, harmony, and symmetry with which the master mathematician designed the universe are caught in the lines of light that make the form patterns of the yantras and chakras (wheels that signify the constant and dynamic circulation of the power of the Infinite).

One can contemplate the Absolute as a mass of ineffable light but if one wants to see the actual form of one's favorite deity, the light has to be codified into a definite pattern of rays; this codification is exactly what the rishis proceeded to do. This type of yantra limits the limitless into a geometrical figure drawn with lines, circles, squares, and triangles. Due to its mathematical precision, such a yantra is a powerhouse of cosmic energy. Within its concrete form it encloses the uncontrollable power of the deity that it is meant to represent. It creates a field of power that lives, breathes, and moves with life, and within which the power of the Divine can be invoked. These forms have always existed in the etheric sphere but we, with our limited vision, are unable to perceive them. The rishis drew them out of the vast ocean of consciousness that holds within it all conceivable forms. The forms we see in Nature are only their gross representations and rest on the subtle forms given by the yantras.

The mystic power of yantras has been narrated in many sacred books. In the *Shiva Mahapurana* Lord Shiva explains to his consort Parvati that a yantra is as essential to the worship of the gods as a body is essential for living beings and oil to oil lamps. A yantra is helpful in every field of life: to attain success in one's profession, to acquire wealth, to find peace, to bring good luck, to get rid of tensions, to ward off diseases, and to progress in meditation. By keeping a potentized yantra in a sacred place in one's house and worshipping it daily, one can fulfill all desires and attain all goals.

The focal point of a yantra is always the *bindu* or center. It represents the point, nucleus, or seed from which creation has evolved and into which it will return. It also represents the union of the two dual principles of the universe, Shiva and Shakti—Consciousness and Energy. It can be called the point of contact between the creator and his creation. It is the drop that swells into the ocean of pure consciousness. It is the cipher by which everything else is deciphered.

Most yantras make use of many forms. The circle is a primal form. Even our earth is in the form of a circle. The circle represents the cycle of timelessness, which has no beginning and no end. It denotes eternity and points to the eternal cycle of birth, existence, and death. Space cannot be circumscribed by anything less than three lines, so the next form used in yantras is the triangle. The square denotes the terrestrial and physical world that is to be transcended. It is the substratum on which the yantra rests. The lotus is a flower that responds only to the call of light. It raises its head when the sun rises and closes its petals when it sets. The flower opens out, petal by petal, which signifies the gradual unfolding of the latent spirituality in us. This is why the symbol of the lotus holds an important place in all the chakras, which are also yantras.

Sri Chakra

The Sri Chakra is known as the king of all chakras. It is the most potent and famous of all yantras. The Sri Chakra is also known as the Sri Yantra and is the most complex figure used for worship, devotion, and meditation. It has been in use for thousands of years and its origin is unknown. It contains all other chakras within it, as the Divine Mother goddess contains all other gods and goddesses within her. By worshipping the Sri Chakra, one can worship any of the other gods or goddesses. The central figure is composed of nine interlocking triangles. Modern mathematicians are astounded by the beauty and symmetry of this incredible figure, the secret of which they have still not been able to fathom.

A few attempts at drawing this figure will make it obvious that it is not as easy as it looks. Every triangle is connected to the others by common points and this is the reason why it is so difficult to make a perfect reproduction of this yantra. Changing the size or position of one triangle changes the position of many other triangles, which will end in total confusion. Given the fact that this is one of the oldest and most recognizable figures of the sacred geometry of the Hindus, one would assume that a correct method for drawing this legendary figure would be easy to find. But this is not so. The two most famous methods, which are normally used, are not very precise. Many modern techniques have been tried but after a careful scrutiny of all the figures, one realizes that they are all different! Was there an original geometrical figure that had been distorted with time? This mystery is still to be solved.

The bindu or dot is considered to be the navel of the Sri Chakra. The bindu becomes the triangle and the triangle expands into the eight-sided figure, then to a ten-cornered figure, and so on. Thus, the bindu or dot of the primary triangle transforms itself through a series of lines, triangles, circles, and squares to the fully formed shape of the Sri Chakra. The vibrations that emanate from the Sri Chakra are so positive that even a person who sits near it is subtly influenced by it. Adi Shankara, the founder of Advaita Vedanta, installed the Sri Chakra in all the temples that he visited or established all over India.

Yantra Construction

During some types of *pujas* or rituals, yantras are made on the floor using various colored powders like rice, turmeric, and vermilion. However, yantras and chakras are normally made out of certain types of metals like copper, silver, and gold. Modern science has found out that it is possible to generate heat and magnetic waves by channeling energy or electricity through copper coils. The "sim card" in a mobile phone is only a small, flat piece of very thin copper. By applying electrical charges to the card, we can store millions of data bits in the form of sounds and visuals. Even more amazing is the fact that you can use this sim card in another mobile phone to reproduce the same information even after many years. Thus, modern science has at last discovered that we can transform letters, words, and pictures into sounds and these frequencies can later be changed back into letters and words!

This is something our rishis had discovered ages ago and the yantras are their contribution to humankind to enable them to obtain spiritual benefits. The rishis knew that metals like gold, copper, and silver are the best for conducting electrical charges. Thus, they made their yantras out of these three materials. These plates act like the printed circuit board of a computer. They also had symbols to represent different sounds of the universe, which were incorporated into the yantras.

The priest then charged the yantras by mentally chanting the mantras and thus used the biocurrents generated in their own bodies to transmit the desired message to the metal plates. At the same time they also touched certain objects like wet flowers and leaves, and transferred the invisible energies to the metal plate through their touch. When energy is passed through a copper coil, the metal becomes a magnet. Similarly, when the priest or the devotee constantly repeats this process over a period of time, the metal will be transformed into a cosmic magnet, which is called a yantra.

Nowadays it is common for people to buy yantras and keep them in their houses or wear them as talismans. But it must be understood that unless the spiritual energy in the yantra has been activated, it will not be of much use. Of course the person who has it can also activate the yantra by constant repetition of the mantra and by touching and handling it with a particular intention or *samkalpa* in the mind.

TANTRA:
COMBINING MANTRA AND YANTRA

The rishis dissected the human personality and developed different sciences to raise it to its highest potential. Along with the process of using yantras, the rishis also formulated the technique known as *tantra*. Tantra is a mental science—a meta-psychology or method of exploring the mind and developing the range of one's perception. It can be called the science of personality. The human psyche is actually a field of all possibilities. Tantra declares that enlightenment is available to every type of personality—spiritual or sensual, theistic or atheistic, weak or strong. All human emotions like fear, passion, hatred, love, and anger are energy forces. If controlled they can enable us to experience higher realities. The Supreme according to tantra is Adi Shakti, or the Divine Mother, who possesses the ultimate personality. She is the supreme expression of the totality of manifest existence.

The aim of tantra is to replace the limited human personality with an unlimited divine one. Tantra also teaches that by using the name (mantra) and imagining the form of any deity, it is possible to attain the nameless and formless Brahman. Mantra, the sound, and yantra, the form, are both to be used in the path mapped by tantra. Mantra is the energy that moves the vehicle or yantra according to the path as prescribed by tantra. The best yantra is the human body. The Divine already resides within this body and if certain tantric rites are performed, the individual will be able to reach his or her full divine potential. The highest Self is said to be a priceless gem locked in a chest that is buried in mud. Tantric disciplines consist in clearing the mud of our petty, negative desires and opening the treasure box in our brain to expose the gem of self-awareness.

The universe, including our own bodies, has evolved out of the Shakti or Energy of Pure Consciousness, which is known in tantra as Shiva. Although Shiva and Shakti have momentarily parted in order to create the world, they are forever striving to unite in the human body in order to experience cosmic unity. The whole aim of tantra is to attain this cosmic union. Thus, tantra insists that every experience that comes to the individual, whether good or bad, should be accepted gratefully. The universe is a manifestation of Shakti, the Divine Mother, so everything that takes place in the universe is also divine. Tantric sadhana is also used for procuring material benefits since they are the foundation on which the whole spiritual structure stands.

Our body contains invisible sound transmitters and receivers. When sound waves exceed a certain range, our ears are no longer able to hear them. However, we hold within us the ability to hear these sounds, which are constantly coming from the etheric sphere. This is how the ancient rishis heard the Vedic hymns. With meditation and pranayama (breath control), and the use of mantras and yantras, the body will acquire the capacity to hear these sounds. Think how powerful we can be if we integrate our mind with cosmic sound.

However, tantra is a difficult path, which has to be learned only from a proficient guru who has mastered the techniques; otherwise it might have dangerous consequences.

Mudras and Other Symbols

The rishis explored every method (all of them scientific) by which the human being could surmount the obstacles on the spiritual path and attain union with the Divine. Another method used is that of mystic hand symbols, known as *mudras,* which invoke the power of the deity and activate the mantra. The mudras are made by pressing the thumb to the tips of different fingers and thus invoking the energy residing in our body. The tips of the fingers contain many nerves that go directly to certain parts of the body. These mudras are a kind of sign language that is understood by the body; they cause it to react in a certain way.

Hinduism also uses many concrete symbols, such as the *svastika,* an ancient symbol from India now found all over the world. The name comes from the Sanskrit words *svasti* (well-being) and *asti* (is). It is a symbol for bringing good fortune and well-being. The right-handed svastika is one of the 108 symbols of the God Vishnu as well as a symbol of the sun god, Surya. The rotation of its arms toward the right indicates the course taken daily by the sun. Interestingly, this is a symbol for the sun among Native Americans also. The left-handed form of the svastika, which is called *sauvastika,* is sometimes considered to be evil since it represents night, black magic, and the Goddess Kali. However, it is the form most commonly used in Buddhism. Strangely enough, this is the symbol that Hitler used for the Nazi movement.

Scientifically Based Worship

Puja is a ritualistic method of worshipping the gods. It aims at the accomplishment of some intention or desire. All pujas have a scientific basis. Hindus do pujas in their houses and also in temples; many of us can certify that they produce the desired effect. How is this possible? The *samkalpa* or intention is what shapes the end product. It is mentally made by us when the *pujari* (priest) asks us to touch the plate in which the flowers to be used for the puja are kept.

When our mind holds a strong samkalpa or intention, it has the effect of actually being able to change the future! This is the very basis of all miracles. Sometimes we find that a doctor pronounces a patient to be incurable and the patient recovers, sometimes due to the latter's own strong desire to live and sometimes due to the prayers of others. In any puja, it is our samkalpa that ensures the result. No doubt our samkalpa can be enhanced by the spiritual quality of the pujari (the one conducting the puja).

All aspects of the pujas conducted in temples have great scientific meanings behind them. They give great benefit to those who participate in them and take the *prasad* (offerings to the deity), which is distributed to all those who are present. This prasad is filled with positive vibrations. At the end of the puja, the consecrated water is sprinkled on the heads of the people who are gathered there and a few drops are also given to them to sip. This water has amazing power.

Water is used in all pujas because water is the best conductor of spiritual vibrations. Even Christian churches have holy water. The consecrated water in temples known as *charanamritam* (nectar of the Lord's feet) is the water that has been poured over the deity to the chanting of mantras. A Japanese scientist has recently proven that the molecules of water undergo a drastic change and attain a high degree of coherence when positive vibrations are passed through them. Our ancient scientists, the rishis, were well aware of this fact. Hence, this charanamritam has a very strong effect on the person who drinks it. Even the Hindus themselves do not realize that this is not just any water but water that has been potentized with mantras. The molecular structure of this water is totally different from ordinary water that has not been treated.

SACRED SCIENCE OF DAILY LIFE

The rishis knew many esoteric truths, which are only recently being discovered by scientists. We often fail to realize the scientific nature of many aspects that are interwoven into the daily life of the Hindu. The rishis implanted a spiritual seed in every action of the human being and thus Hinduism is more a way of life than a religion. The life of a true Hindu is spiritualism put into practice. If we follow the rules set forth by the rishis for a good life, we will find that every one of them has a scientific basis and is meant to take us to the fulfillment of a perfect life.

For example, the first thing that a Hindu is supposed to do when he or she gets up is to touch the earth with the fingers and repeat a certain mantra to the earth goddess, *Vishnu patnir namasthubhyam, padasparsham kshamasvame:* "O thou consort of Vishnu, please forgive my transgressions on thee." There are two important reasons for this. One is to remind us of the great duty we owe to the earth—our very first mother. We ask her forgiveness for stamping on her, digging in her, and performing all the hundreds of dreadful things we do. Another reason is that the poles within our body need to be earthed when we wake up and this small act does just that.

When we take our bath, we are also asked to chant a certain mantra. By repeating this mantra, which has positive vibrations, the negative qualities of the water are removed. The same applies to the food we eat. We are told to chant certain mantras and circle the food with water held in our palms and then sprinkle some of that water on the food and drink the rest. It is only now that modern scientists have come to realize that this chanting and sprinkling of the water produces untold benefits.

Let us look at the way Hindus greet each other. They fold their palms together and utter the word *namaste*. The two palms are placed together in front of the chest and the head is bowed when saying this word. Sometimes the eyes are closed. This action of holding the palms together with the tips of the fingers touching each other stimulates the nerve endings, which are connected to various parts of the body. As with mudras, this touching is capable of activating certain points and chakras in the body, thus making us more alert and alive.

The scriptures enjoin five forms of traditional greetings for Hindus and this is the one that is most commonly used. *Namaste* means "I bow to you, or my greetings or prostrations to you." It also is a way of saying, "May our minds meet." When we bow our head, we extend our love with humility. This greeting has a deep spiritual meaning. This is the action we make when we go to the temple. When we do the same action when meeting a person, we are recognizing the fact that the body that stands in front of us is the temple of God, the outer covering of the Divine Spirit, and thus we are greeting or prostrating before that Divine Spirit and not just the gross form of flesh and blood. When we salute another person with this feeling, the very act will take us to spiritual heights of communion with the Divine and inspire a feeling of love in the other person.

In olden times, every Hindu used to use a dot or some other mark in the center of his or her forehead, marking the *ajna chakra* (third eye), the seat of intelligence. When we meet a person wearing such a dot, our eyes are immediately drawn to the middle of his or her forehead. The other person will have a similar experience and thus each will be able to draw the best from the other since they are both concentrating on the third eye. Thus, even this cosmetic and perhaps insignificant aspect of Hinduism has a scientific basis.

In south India, when Hindus go to a Ganesha temple, they hold their earlobes with opposite hands and bob up and down in front of the idol of Ganesha. This exercise has recently been discovered to have amazing health benefits, since the lobes of the ears contain a number of nerves, which stimulate the brain centers. The act of going up and down also greases the knees and elbows and keeps them supple.

Since olden days it has been the custom to light a lamp daily before the altar of the Lord. In some houses it is lit twice a day, at dawn and dusk. All auspicious functions commence with the lighting of the lamp, which is kept lit throughout the occasion. Light symbolizes knowledge. The Lord is *chaitanya* or the light of all knowledge. Hence light is worshipped as the Lord himself. The question may be asked as to why we should not light an electric bulb instead of an oil lamp. That will also remove darkness. But as with all things in Hinduism, the traditional oil or ghee lamp has a symbolic and therefore spiritual significance. The wick stands for our ego and the oil or ghee for our negative tendencies, both inherited and acquired. When we light the lamp, we pray that our negative tendencies, enmity to others, and so on should be removed. When the ego is touched by the light of spiritual knowledge, the negative tendencies slowly exhaust themselves as the oil becomes less and less. This daily affirmation by the mind has the effect of imperceptibly eradicating negativity. Western psychology has come to recognize positive affirmations as one of the best methods of treatment. Moreover, ghee has the power to purify the environment when it is lit.

The Western mind considered Nature, God, and human to be totally unconnected. The rishis, on the other hand, realized that these three are actually interconnected and what affects one part will affect every other part. If Nature is defiled, we will have to suffer, which is what is happening to us now. Every thought and action of the human being has a deep impact on the universe as a whole. Thus, the rishis insisted that deep consideration should be shown to Nature. Nature or Prakriti is not inert matter to be used and misused according to our pleasure, but a pulsating, living being, which needs to be treated with all consideration and love. Only then will she yield her resources to the human being.

> *When the mind is detached from memory, perception*
> *gets total clarity. It gives correct and complete knowledge,*
> *beyond which nothing remains to be known.*
> *The yogic mind abides in total silence. In supreme silence*
> *the mind is liberated from the world of change to rest in*
> *unbounded consciousness.*
>
> PATANJALI, *YOGA SUTRAS*

He who knows the first vital thread,

Binding all things formed in shape, color, and words,

Knows only the physical form of the universe, and knows
*   very little of that,*

But he who goes deeper and perceives the string inside the
*   string,*

The thin web binding separate life forces with the cords of
*   unity,*

Knows the real entity.

Only he knows truly the mighty omnipotent and
*   omnipresent God,*

Who is within and beyond all formulated entities of the
*   vast universe,*

Penetrate deeper to know the ultimate truth.

ATHARVA VEDA

Loka Samasthath Sukhino Bhavantu!

Satchidanandaaya Namaha!
Salutations to the One Who Is Existence-Consciousness-Bliss!

13

The Goals of Sanatana Dharma

Experiential Science of Truth, Goodness, and Peace

Find the eternal object of your quest within your Self,
Enough have you wandered during the long period of
your quest!
Dark and weary must have been the ages of your search
in ignorance,
And groping in helplessness.
At last when you turn your gaze inward, suddenly you
realize that the
Bright light of faith and lasting truth was shining
around you.
With rapturous joy, you find the soul of the universe,

202

The eternal object of your quest.
Your searching mind at last finds the object of the
  search,
Within your own heart.

YAJUR VEDA

He whom they call in the Vedanta as One Person,
  pervading both worlds,
Whose title "Lord" applies to no other,
For whom the seekers of deliverance search within their
  vital breaths,
Who is found with ease through the yoga of devotion,
May he, the Absolute Lord, lead you to the supreme
  good.

SHIVA PURANA

Many civilizations have come into existence in some small region of the world and perished in the course of time. But Hindu culture or Sanatana Dharma has existed from the dawn of time, unparalleled, retaining its inherent values through the ages. Based on dharma, the cosmic law of righteousness, it has persisted through many invasions and attacks. For a thousand years previous to the British Raj, foreign marauders repeatedly attempted to destroy Hinduism through overt physical genocide and the systematic destruction of Hindu temples and sacred places. Our sages and warriors fought bravely to stem this anti-Hindu holocaust to the best of their ability, often paying for their bravery with their lives. Then, during the last century, the classical, traditional Hinduism that had been responsible for the continuous development of thousands of years of a unique culture, architecture, music, philosophy, ritual, and theology came under a devastating assault that was different from any other it had faced in the past.

THE BRITISH COLONIAL ASSAULT
ON SANATANA DHARMA

India was the richest country in the world till the advent of the British in the seventeenth century. The personal wealth amassed by Robert Clive alone from the plunder of Bengal was £401,102. The total amount of treasure looted from India by the British had reached one billion pounds by 1901. And this total does not include the value of the Kohinoor diamond. Apart from this financial catastrophe, there was another tragic occurrence during the nineteenth century, the destructive magnitude of which Hindu leaders and scholars are only dimly beginning to recognize and assess. This development both altered and weakened Hinduism to a tremendous degree.

What the Hindu community experienced under British Christian domination was an ominous form of cultural genocide. It was a subtle yet systematic program of intellectual and spiritual annihilation. It is easy to defend oneself from the threat of an enemy who tries to kill one physically, but much harder to recognize the threat of an enemy who outwardly claims to serve the best interests of the people that it has subjugated while slowly seeking to undermine the authority of its cultural heritage!

As soon as they came to India, the British had recognized that the dignity, strength, and beauty of traditional Hinduism were the foremost threat to Christian European rule in India. This is an extract from Macaulay's address to the British Parliament on February 2, 1835.

I have traveled across the length and breadth of India and I have not seen one person who is a beggar or who is a thief. Such wealth have I seen in this country, such high moral values, people of such caliber that I do not think we would ever conquer this country, unless we break the very backbone of this nation, which is her spiritual and cultural heritage and therefore, I propose that we replace her old and ancient education system and her culture, for if the Indians can be made to think that all that is foreign and English is good and greater than their own, they will lose their self-esteem, their native culture, and they will become what we want them to be, a truly dominated nation!

This is exactly what the British proceeded to do. They set out to systematically destroy our spiritual wealth, which is also the basis of our scientific knowledge, and thus impoverished the whole nation into becoming a set of poor imitators and docile servants of the British Raj. The British did not overtly destroy temples or desecrate Hindu art. Their attempts were more subtle. The unfortunate part was that this attempt was aided by the Hindu intelligentsia, who were desperate to get into the good books of their conquerors. Perhaps Annie Besant realized what her own people were doing to the deep-rooted faith and culture of the land they had conquered, and the need for Indians to preserve their culture, when she wrote:

Make no mistake; without Hinduism, India has no future. Hinduism is the soil into which India's roots are struck, and torn of that she will inevitably wither, as a tree torn out from its place. Many are the religions and many are the races flourishing in India, but none of them stretches back into the far dawn of her past, nor are they necessary for her endurance as a nation. Everyone might pass away as they came and India would still remain. But let Hinduism vanish and what is she? A geographical expression of the past, a dim memory of a perished glory, her literature, her art, her monuments, all have Hindudom written across them. If the Hindus do not maintain Hinduism, who shall save it? If India's own children do not cling to her faith, who shall guard it? India alone can save India, and India and Hinduism are one.

In fact, the whole world is really bound to support this ancient religion and to see that its scriptures are kept intact for future generations, for the ancient tenets found in the Vedas and the Upanishads offer liberation from bondage to all humanity. This is why the methods of leading a dharmic life (relating to the laws of righteousness embedded in nature) are slowly creeping into other cultures, even when they do not realize that the foundation of such ideas is in the Sanatana Dharma.

Now the time has come for every Hindu all over the world, regardless whether they were born Hindus or have accepted the faith as their own, to see that this ancient religion and way of life should be kept alive. The ideals of this wonderful dharma should be spread all over the world in as systematic a manner as Westerners sought to suppress it during the nineteenth and twentieth centuries. Just as the Indians of those times were enticed to view their own culture as outdated and encouraged to ape Western culture, so now the science of Sanatana Dharma needs to be shared with other noble-minded souls everywhere.

THE SPIRITUAL BASIS OF SURVIVING AND THRIVING

The basis of all Hindu scientific genius is its spirituality. That is why it has lasted for so long. Great care was taken by all the rishis and saints of India to ensure that a touch of spirituality was injected into every type of human endeavor. Human excellence depends on the development of true cultural values, which are human values.

Hinduism has four goals of life known as *purushaarthas*. They are the pursuit of *dharma* (righteousness), *artha* (material possessions), *kama* (pleasure), and *moksha* (enlightenment). These are the great human values Hinduism has always concentrated on inculcating in society. It has always been ready to accept any activity that strives to increase these values.

The four purushaarthas are like the four wheels of the chariot of the human body. They collectively uphold it and lead it. Each influences the movement of the other three, and in the absence of any one of them, the chariot comes to a halt. These goals cover the whole gamut of human life. The pursuits of wealth and pleasure have not been overlooked in Hinduism, but they are bound on one side by righteousness and on the other side by a desire for liberation. Righteous methods of gaining wealth and pleasure are encouraged in Hinduism since they are basic needs of the human being. That is why Narayana, the Lord who is responsible for the maintenance of the world order, is married to Lakshmi, the goddess of wealth and auspiciousness. If the methods used for gaining wealth and pleasures are righteous, even they will lead to moksha or liberation. This is what Hinduism declares. If the right path is chosen, the correct goal will be reached!

This is part of the wholesome scientific approach to life. It is not easy to reach the goal of enlightenment. All of one's energy should be focused on that goal to assure success. Even in mundane affairs, we find that the artist, scientist, engineer, doctor, or dancer who puts her whole heart and soul into her art or work is the one who is likely to succeed. If this is so for the material world, how much more would it be for the spiritual?

LIVING TRUTH AND NONVIOLENCE

The main message of Hinduism is that of satya and ahimsa—truth and nonviolence. If you look on everything as divine, you can never hurt or harm anything, either in Nature or in the human being. Thus, the Hindu has never wanted to conquer or control anything except his own mind. India has never invaded any country in the last ten thousand years of its history. This is the best accolade that can be given to this culture and one that shows its uniqueness.

Traditional Hinduism has always been the most tolerant, patient, and welcoming of all religions. It has never persecuted others merely because they had a different theological belief. Hinduism has always sought to live side-by-side peacefully with the followers of other religions, whether they were the indigenous Indian religions of Buddhism, Jainism, and Sikhism or the foreign religions of Christianity and Islam. Hindu India has been the sole nation on earth where the Jewish community has never been persecuted even though they have been living here for more than two thousand years. Similarly, Zoroastrian refugees escaping the destruction of the Persian civilization at the hands of Islamic conquerors were warmly welcomed in India more than a thousand years ago. The Zoroastrian community (now known as the Parsis) has thrived and lived amicably with their Hindu neighbors in peace and mutual respect. Recently when China overran Tibet, India was the only country who gave asylum to the Dalai Lama and allowed the Tibetans to come and settle down on Indian soil without hindrance, with freedom to practice their own religion—Buddhism.

A UNIQUE VISION

The mistake that is now being made by modern Hindus, especially those living abroad, is to confuse the long-held Hindu tradition of tolerating other religions with the notion that Hinduism encourages us to believe that all religions are exactly the same. The leap from tolerance of other faiths to a belief that all religions are equal is not a leap that is grounded in logic. Nor is it grounded in the history, literature, or philosophy of the Hindu tradition itself.

Hinduism is its own uniquely independent religious tradition, different and distinct from any other religion on earth. This distinction has been asserted by all our great saints. The great Hindu saints used to have debates with the protagonists of non-Hindu traditions like Buddhism, Jainism, and Charvakins (atheists). The sages of Hinduism met all philosophical challenges and succeeded in defeating their philosophical opponents in open assemblies. Adi Shankaracharya, founder of Advaita Vedanta, went all over the peninsula, defeating all his learned opponents in open debate. This was known as his "Digvijaya," or "Conquest of all Directions." Indeed, Shankara is attributed as being partially responsible for the decline of Buddhism in India, due to his great ability in debate by which he totally annihilated his opponents' arguments and proved the superiority of the Vedantic doctrines.

The great teacher Madhvacharya, founder of the Dvaita school of Vedanta, is similarly seen as being responsible for the sharp decline of Jainism in south India due to his acute intelligence and great debating skills in defense of the Vaidika Dharma (Vedic Dharma). All premodern Hindu sages and philosophers recognized and celebrated the singularly unique vision that Hinduism has to offer the world. They clearly distinguished between Hindu and non-Hindu religions, and they defended Hinduism to the utmost of their formidable intellectual and spiritual abilities. They did so unapologetically, professionally, and courageously. The Hindu worldview makes sense and will survive only if we celebrate Hinduism's uniqueness today.

AUM PEACE! PEACE! PEACE!

Let us listen to the voice of the great rishis, exhorting us to look to the Divine within us and see it everywhere so that the world can live in true love and compassion for the whole of the whole universe and for the creatures that live in it. We can be guided by the great Vedic prayer for universal peace.

> *Aum svasti prajabhyaam, paripaalayantaam,*
> *Nyayena margena, mahimahishaha,*
> *Go brahmanebhyam shubamastu nityam,*
> *Lokaasamstaa sukhino bhavantu.*

> May all people be happy,
> May the kings rule the earth righteously,
> Let animals and men of wisdom be taken care of,
> May everyone be filled with auspiciousness.

> *Kaale varshatu parjanyaha,*
> *Prithivi shashyashaalini,*
> *Deshoyam kshobharahitaha,*
> *Satjanaath santu nirbhayaaha.*

May rains come at the proper time,
May the earth produce all types of grain,
May countries be free from famine,
May good people be free from fear.

Sarveshaam svastir bhavatu,
Sarveshaam shantir bhavatu,
Sarvesham poornam bhavatu,
Sarvesham mangalam bhavatu,
Sarve bhavantu sukhinaha,
Sarve santu niraamayaaha,
Sarve bhadraani pashyantu,
Ma kaschid dukhabhav bhaveth.
Aum Shanti! Shanti! Shantihi!

Let the whole world enjoy good health,
Let the whole world enjoy peace,
Let the whole world enjoy prosperity,
Let the whole world be filled with auspiciousness,
May all creatures be happy,
May everybody be free from disease,
May all see only auspiciousness in everything,
Let not any sorrow prevail.
Aum Peace! Peace! Peace!

Truth, eternal order, that is great and stern,
Consecrations, austerity, prayer, and ritual uphold the earth.
May she, queen of what has been and will be, care and
provide vast space for us.

                                        Atharva Veda

Loka Samasthath Sukhino Bhavantu!

ॐ

Poems to India

Verses Composed by Vanamali

How fortunate am I to be born a Hindu on this holy
　　soil,
Breathing the perfumed air, saturated by the breath of
　　countless sages,
Drinking in the sight of this sacred river,
This incredible mountain,
Listening to the chants of the ages,
Washed down the river of time,
Floating across the Ganga,
Bells ringing, conches blaring,
The sound of Aum, echoing down the corridors of time,
Thrilling me to the very core,
Urging me not to waste even a small precious moment,
Charging me to go forward,
Searching for my ephemeral self,
Which all the time resides in me,
My constant companion,
My lover of a thousand ages,
My child, my father, my mother, my beloved,

My one and only Me,
The eternal Me,
Nothing else exists,
There is no Thou,
Only I, I, and again I.

O to be in India when the monsoons come,
To feel the rain on your face, the mist in your eyes,
To smell the earth with heaving bosom,
To bow before the lashing waters,
To laugh with the thunder and gurgle with the stream,
To flinch when the lightning hits your eyes,
To listen bemused to the orchestra of the night,
To be in India—to be an Indian!

When will I be able to roam over the Himalayas,
The cradle of our culture,
To be young and free and clamber over the snowy
    mountains,
To feel my Mother's pulse rushing in my veins,
To feel her spirit raising me to the heights,
To plumb the depths of her beauty,
To unveil the secret of her eternity,
To roam wild over her mountainside,
To plunge into the depths of her waters,
To rejoice that the eternal spirit of the rishis
Courses through my veins,
To be free, to be a seeker,
To be an Indian!

Himalaya!

Thy name is a blessing and a boon,

Walking through the forest of Devatarus—the trees of
the gods,

I sit sometimes immobile, meditating on thee O mighty
Himalaya!

To think of thee is to be blessed!

To live in thee is grace supreme,

To die on thy chest is liberation!

O Ganga!

Thou art not a river,

Thou art a goddess,

Coursing through the Milky Way of stars,

Washing the feet of Vishnu,

Falling on the matted locks of Shambu,

Beguiled by Bhageeratha,

Gushing down the gorges of the Himalayas,

Rushing through the plains,

To defile the purity of your waters in the salty ocean,

In order to bless this land, the land of your choice.

O Ganga! Thou ethereal goddess,

Blessed am I to have thy darshana every morning!

How fortunate am I to be born on this holy land,

Where countless sages and gods have trod,

Where the very air is fragrant with the perfume of
their holy feet,

Where sacred rivers and streams gush in ecstasy to
reach the ocean,

Where every stone is a linga in disguise,

Where every cow is a holy animal,
Where one can lie on the earth and say,
This is my land, the holy land.

Love lies in the heart of the sun,
You cannot see it but you can feel its heat,
Soaking through you, filling you with warmth,
It reveals itself in the eyes of the person before you,
Even though you might never have seen him before.
It shines through the twinkling gaze of your child,
Who looks at you as if you were the end and the all.
It enters your heart unattended,
Ready to reveal itself, ready to care for you,
If you allow it.
All the love you get in the world is the love of god
    for you,
The love of you (the human) for god!
There is no other love—there is no other love.

However many births I might take,
May I still be born a Hindu,
As a tulsi leaf or lotus flower,
On the soil of India,
How many births have I gone through,
As leaf and worm and reptile—animal and brute man,
Before being born a Hindu on this sacred soil.
My Mother, Supreme!
I take thy sacred dust and place it reverently on
    my head,
I am replete with thy love, thy compassion.

Mother allow me to serve you till the end of my life.
Take my hand Mother and lead me to liberation.

There is a divine romance flowering in the hearts of all,
An aroma of the spirit, creeping into our souls,
A mystic sound emanating from our hearts,
Prepare yourselves O daughters and sons of this soil,
The dawn is about to break!

Glossary
of Sanskrit Terms

aranya: Pertaining to the forest

acharya: Teacher

adharmic: Unrighteous

Aditi: Mother of the gods

advaita: Nondual

agni: Fire

ahamtva: Ego sense of I

ahara shuddhi: Purity of food

ahimsa: Nonviolence

ajna chakra: The chakra between the brows

akasa: Sky (space)

amavasya: New moon day

anadi: That which has no beginning

ananda: Bliss

anandamaya kosha: The sheath of bliss

ananta: That which has no end

annamaya kosha: The sheath of food

anu: Atom

apah: The element of water

apana: The breath that is exhaled

apara vidya: Scientific knowledge

apas: Water

apaurusheya: Not the work of human beings

aranya: Pertaining to the forest

aric: Wise man; sage

artha: Wealth

asaana: Approximate

asana: A seat

asat: Nonexistence

ashrama: Spiritual retreat

ashtanga yoga: The yoga of eight limbs, of Patanjali

asti: Beingness

asura: Demonic being

atma(n): The divine spirit in the human being

Aum: The initial sound of the cosmos

avaidika: Contrary to the Veda

avatara: Incarnation of God

avidya: Ignorance

avyakta: That which is not clear

bhakta: Devotee

bhakti marga: The path of devotion

bhakti yoga: The yoga of devotion

bilva/vilva: Type of leaf important in the worship of Shiva

bindu: Dot

braahmana: A brahmin; a member of the highest class

brahamanda: A supergalaxy

brahma muhurtam: Time between 3 and 4 am

brahmacharya: Celibacy

brahmajnana: Knowledge of Brahman

brahmanishta rishi: Sage who is established in Brahman

brahmarishi: Sage who is a knower of Brahman

briha: Large

chaitanya: light of divine consciousness

chakra: wheel

chandas: Meter used in hymns

Chandogya: One of the Upanishads

chikitsa vijnana: Knowledge of treatments

chit, chitta, chid: Highest level of the mind; consciousness

chitta shuddhi: Purification of the mind

chitta vritti nirodha: To steady the wavering mind

Daksha: One of the patriarchs; he was born out of the right thumb of Brahma, the Creator

dama: Self-restraint

dana: Charity

darshana: Point of view

daya: Compassion

desha: Country

deva: Shining one (god)

dhamanis: Veins and nerves that supply food to the body

dharma: Universal law of life and righteousness

Dharma Shastra: Book describing the duties of a human being

dharmic: Pertaining to dharma

dhatu: Nerve

dhruva: A type of grass used in worship of Ganesha

doshas: The three problems of the body

dravya vijnana: Pharmacology

dvaita: Duality

gada: Mace

gayatri: Name of a meter; famous hymn to the sun god

gotra: Lineage coming from a rishi

gotra pravartakas: Founders of the brahmanical clans

gotra rishi: Rishi whose name was given to a lineage

gunas: The three strands of Nature

guru: Spiritual preceptor

homa: Fire ceremony

ishta deva: Favorite deity

Itihasa: Epic

jadaragni: Fire of digestion

jagat: World

jagrita: Waking state of consciousness

japa: Repetition of god's name

japa yoga: The yoga of the repetition of a mantra

jijnasu: Inquirer on the path of truth

jiva: The life principle

jivatma: The embodied soul

jnana: Wisdom

jnana kanda: Volume or portion pertaining to wisdom

jnana marga: The path of wisdom

jnani: Person of wisdom

jyestha: Elder

jyotisha: Astrology

kaala: Time

Kali Yuga: Name of the present epoch

kalpa: Lifetime of Brahma, the creator

kama: Passion; pleasure; desire

kapha: Phlegm; one of the three doshas

karma: Action; bonds accruing from action

karma kanda: Volume or portion pertaining to action

karmic: Pertaining to the bonds created by action

krimis: Germs; parasites; worms

krishna paksha: Dark half of the lunar month

kurma: Tortoise

laya: State of dissolution

lila: Play

loka: World

lokasamgraham: For the maintenance of the world

mahakashayas: Herbal concoctions used in Ayurveda

maharishi: Great sage

mahavakyas: The great sayings of the Upanishads

mala: Necklace

mamatva: Sense of mineness

mandala: Mystic drawing

mandukam: Frog

mantra: A spiritual formula

mantra drashta: The person to whom a mantra was revealed

manvantara: An epoch ruled by a Manu

matsya: Fish

matsya yantra: An instrument using the fish symbol

maya: The illusion of a separate world; appearance; the phenomenal world

meena: An astrological sign

meru: Mythical peak

mesha: Astrological sign and the name of a month

mesha sankranthi: The day preceeding the month called Mesha

mesha sankranthi rekha: The Alpha Aries point from which the earth starts its rotation around the sun

mesha vishuvath: Hindu new year

mithya: That which does not exist

moksha: Liberation from mortal coils

mudra: Mystic sign made by joining the thumb to one of the fingers

muladhara chakra: Energy whorl found at the base of the spine

Mundaka: Name of one Upanishad

nadi: A nerve

Nadi Shastra: A form of Indian astrology in which people's horoscopes are recorded on palm leaves

nakshatra: Star

nama: Name

namaste: Folding the palms together as a salutation; verbal greeting, meaning "I bow to you or my greetings or prostrations to you"

Narasimha: The incarnation of Vishnu as half-human and half-lion

nav: Boat

navagatih: Navigation

neti, neti: Not this, not this

nimisha: Second

nimitta: Cause

nirukta: Etymology

ojas: Physical splendor

padaas: Steps

pakayantras: Laboratory instruments

pancha bhutas: The five elements in Nature

pancha karmas: The five types of cleansing in Ayurveda

pancha mahabhutas: The five great elements

papa: Sin

para vidya: Knowledge of the Absolute

paramanu: Molecule

Paramatma: The Supreme Soul

patrika: Palm leaves on which horoscopes were written

pitta: Bile; one of the three doshas

poorna: Totally full

poorva janma: Previous birth

prajnanaghanam: Filled with consciousness

Prakriti: Nature

pralaya: Flood

pramaana: Infallible knowledge

prana: Vital breath; life-force

pranamaya kosha: The sheath of breath around the body

pranava mantra: The mantra Aum

pranava svaroopa: The form of Aum

pranayama: The technique of breath control

pranic: Pertaining to the prana or life-force

prarabdha karma: Results of action done in a previous life

prasad: Leftover of offerings to God

prasna: Inquiry

pratibha: Highly developed intuition

prithvi: The earth

puja: Ritualistic worship of God

punya: Spiritual merit

punya kaalam: Auspicious time

puranic: Pertaining to the Puranas

puranic rishis: The sages responsible for writing the Puranas

Purusha: The Supreme Person

rajas: Activity, passion; one of the three modes of Nature

renu: Particle

rik: Hymn from the Rig Veda

rishi: Great sage

rudraksha: Seed of a tree that is important to Shiva

rupa: Form

sabda pramana: Vedic hymns (refers to the samhita portion of the Vedas)

sadhana: Spiritual practice

samadhi: Superconscious state

samans: Hymns of the Sama Veda

samhara: Dissolution

samyama: Unbroken mental absorption

samyoga: Union of the jivatma with the Paramatma

Sanatana Dharma: The real name for Hinduism; the ancient or eternal law of righteousness

sandal: Sandalwood

sandhya: That time when day changes to night and night to day

sannyasins: Renunciates who wear ochre robes

saptarishis: The seven sages

sat: Existence

sat-chit-ananda: Existence-consciousness bliss; explanation for Brahman

sattva: Quality of purity; one of the three modes of Nature

satyam: Truth

sauvastika: Left-handed form of the svastika

shad darshanas: Six schools of Hindu philosophy

Shakti: Force, power of the goddess

shalya tantra: Surgical procedures

shastra: Scripture

shloka: Couplet in a poem

shrishti: Creation

shruti: That which was heard (refers to the hymns or Samhita portion of the Vedas)

shruti siras: The head of the Vedas (refers to the Upanishads)

shukla paksha: Bright fortnight of the lunar month

shunya: Zero; nil

siddha: Perfected being

siddhi: Supernormal power

smriti: That which is recollected, the second and third portions of the Vedas

sthiti: Status quo

sushupti: State of deep sleep

svapna: Dreaming state

svara: Pitch

svasti: Auspiciousness; well-being

svastika: A symbol of auspiciousness

svayamvara: Marriage by choice of the bride

tamas: Sleep; inertia; one of the three modes of Nature

tantra: An esoteric type of yoga

tantric: Pertaining to tantra

tapas; tapasya: Austerity

tejas: Spiritual effulgence

tulasi: The holy basil

turiya: State of superconsciousness

upadhis: Conditionings of the mind (space time and causation)

vac: Sound; speech

vaidika: Pertaining to the Vedas

vaidika dharma: Rules of behavior given by the Vedas

Vamana: Incarnation of Vishnu as a dwarf

Varaha: Incarnation of Vishnu as a boar

vata: Element of wind in the body (one of the three doshas)

vayu: Air

Veda: The four holy books of the Hindus

Veda Vedya: That which is to be known through a study of the Veda (referring to Brahman)

Vedic: Pertaining to the Vedas

vel: Spear (weapon used by Lord Subramania)

vidya: Knowledge

vijnanamaya kosha: The intellectual sheath of the human being

vishuvath: The start of the Hindu year

vyakarna: Grammar

vyakta: Perceivable to the senses

vyoma: Transcendental space

yaj: To worship

yajna shalaas: Places where yajnas are held

yajnas: Fire ceremonies

yakrut: Liver

yam: To control

yantra: Instrument, spiritual design

yoga: Spiritual practices to attain union with the Divine

Yoga Sutras: Aphorisms given by the sage Patanjali

yogi: One who practices yoga

yojana: About a mile

yuga: An epoch

yuj: To unite

Bibliography

Capra, Fritjof. *The Tao of Physics*. New York: Fontana, 1976.

McTaggart, Lynn. *The Field*. New York: Harper Collins, 2003.

Mukundcharandas, Sadhu. *Rishis, Mystics and Heroes of India*. Ahmedabad, India: Swaminarayan Aksharpith, 2011.

Panda, N.C. *Maya in Physics*. Delhi: Motilal Banarasidass, 2005.

Saraswati, Sri Chandrashekharendra (Shankaracharya of Kanchi Kamakoti Peetham). *The Vedas*. Mumbai: Bharatiya Vidya Bhavan, 1991.

Vidyalankar, Pandit Satyakam. *The Holy Vedas*. Delhi: Clarion Books, 1998.

Index

BOOKS OF RELATED INTEREST

The Complete Life of Rama
Based on Valmiki's *Ramayana* and the Earliest Oral Traditions
by Vanamali

Shiva
Stories and Teachings from the Shiva Mahapurana
by Vanamali

The Complete Life of Krishna
Based on the Earliest Oral Traditions and the Sacred Scriptures
by Vanamali

Hanuman
The Devotion and Power of the Monkey God
by Vanamali

Shakti
Realm of the Divine Mother
by Vanamali

Chakras
Energy Centers of Transformation
by Harish Johari

The Heart of Yoga
Developing a Personal Practice
by T. K. V. Desikachar

The Practice of Nada Yoga
Meditation on the Inner Sacred Sound
by Baird Hersey

INNER TRADITIONS • BEAR & COMPANY
P.O. Box 388
Rochester, VT 05767
1-800-246-8648
www.InnerTraditions.com

Or contact your local bookseller